PRIDE AND PREJUDICE

"It is a truth well known to all the world that an unmarried man in possession of a large fortune must be in need of a wife." And so, when such a man comes to live near the Bennet family, Mrs. Bennet is delighted. At once, she sees in Mr. Bingley a possible, almost a certain, husband for one of her five daughters.

"People say he's quite young, very handsome, and extremely charming!" says foolish Lydia, the youngest of the Bennet sisters. "And even better, he loves dancing! Everybody knows that means he's likely to fall in love!"

But with whom? Soon, Elizabeth Bennet is sure that he admires her eldest sister, Jane. Certainly, he is most attentive to her whenever they meet, but who can tell if admiration will lead to marriage, and happiness?

Mr. Bingley, however, is not the only young man to show interest in the Bennet girls. There is their cousin, the boring Mr. Collins. There are the officers of the regiment—the charming Mr. Wickham, for example. And of course, there is Mr. Bingley's friend, Mr. Darcy— tall, dark, and extremely wealthy, but then he is such a rude, proud, and disagreeable man . . .

OXFORD BOOKWORMS LIBRARY
Classics

Pride and Prejudice
Stage 6 (2500 headwords)

Series Editor: Jennifer Bassett
Founder Editor: Tricia Hedge
Activities Editors: Jennifer Bassett and Alison Baxter

American Edition: Daphne Mackey, University of Washington

JANE AUSTEN

Pride and Prejudice

Retold by
Clare West

OXFORD UNIVERSITY PRESS

OXFORD
UNIVERSITY PRESS

Great Clarendon Street, Oxford OX2 6DP

Oxford University Press is a department of the University of Oxford.
It furthers the University's objective of excellence in research, scholarship,
and education by publishing worldwide in

Oxford New York

Auckland Cape Town Dar es Salaam Hong Kong Karachi
Kuala Lumpur Madrid Melbourne Mexico City Nairobi
New Delhi Shanghai Taipei Toronto

With offices in

Argentina Austria Brazil Chile Czech Republic France Greece
Guatemala Hungary Italy Japan Poland Portugal Singapore
South Korea Switzerland Thailand Turkey Ukraine Vietnam

OXFORD and OXFORD ENGLISH are registered trade marks of
Oxford University Press in the UK and in certain other countries

ISBN 978 0 19 423762 8

Printed in China

ACKNOWLEDGEMENTS
Illustrated by: Sue Shields

CONTENTS

STORY INTRODUCTION   i

PEOPLE IN THIS STORY   viii

 1 The Bennets' New Neighbor   1

 2 Jane's Illness   9

 3 Mr. Collins Visits Longbourn   19

 4 Elizabeth Meets Mr. Wickham   25

 5 Mr. Collins Proposes Twice   36

 6 Elizabeth Visits Mr. and Mrs. Collins   46

 7 Darcy Proposes Marriage   56

 8 Elizabeth Learns More about Darcy
    and Wickham   65

 9 Elizabeth in Derbyshire   72

10 Lydia and Wickham   81

11 Bingley Returns to Netherfield   90

12 Elizabeth and Darcy   95

    GLOSSARY   105

    ACTIVITIES: Before Reading   108

    ACTIVITIES: While Reading   109

    ACTIVITIES: After Reading   112

    ABOUT THE AUTHOR   116

    ABOUT THE BOOKWORMS LIBRARY   118

PEOPLE IN THIS STORY

Mr. Bennet, *of Longbourn House*
Mrs. Bennet, *his wife*
Jane Bennet ⎫
Elizabeth Bennet ⎪
Mary Bennet ⎬ *their daughters*
Kitty Bennet ⎪
Lydia Bennet ⎭
Charlotte Lucas, *a friend of Elizabeth Bennet's*
Sir William and Lady Lucas, *Charlotte's parents*
Maria Lucas, *Charlotte's sister*
Mr. Collins, *a rector and a distant cousin of Mr. Bennet's*
Mrs. Philips, *Mrs. Bennet's sister*
Mr. Philips, *her husband*
Mr. Gardiner, *Mrs. Bennet's brother*
Mrs. Gardiner, *his wife*

Mr. Charles Bingley, *of Netherfield Park*
Miss Caroline Bingley, *his younger sister*
Mrs. Louisa Hurst, *his elder sister*
Mr. Hurst, *husband to Mrs. Hurst*
Mr. Darcy, *a friend of Mr. Bingley's*
Miss Georgiana Darcy, *Mr. Darcy's young sister*
Colonel Fitzwilliam, *Mr. Darcy's cousin*
Lady Catherine de Bourgh, *Mr. Darcy's aunt*
Miss Anne de Bourgh, *Lady Catherine's daughter*

Mr. George Wickham, *an officer in the regiment*
Colonel Forster, *Commanding Officer of the regiment*
Mrs. Forster, *his wife*

The Bennets' New Neighbor

It is a truth well known to all the world that an unmarried man in possession of a large fortune must be in need of a wife. And when such a man moves into a neighborhood, even if nothing is known about his feelings or opinions, this truth is so clear to the surrounding families that they think of him immediately as the future husband of one or other of their daughters.

"My dear Mr. Bennet," said Mrs. Bennet to her husband one day, "have you heard that someone is going to rent Netherfield Park at last?"

"No, Mrs. Bennet, I haven't," said her husband.

"Don't you want to know *who* is renting it?" cried Mrs. Bennet impatiently.

"You want to tell me, and I don't mind listening."

Mrs. Bennet needed no further encouragement. "Well, my dear, I hear that he's a very rich young man from the north of England. It seems he came to see Netherfield on Monday and was so delighted with it that he arranged to rent it at once. Of course, it *is* the finest house in the area, with the largest gardens. His servants will be here by the end of the week, and *he* will be arriving soon afterwards!"

"What is his name?" asked Mr. Bennet.

"Bingley."

"Is he married or single?"

"Oh, single, my dear, of course! A single man of large fortune—he has an income of four or five thousand pounds a year. How wonderful for our girls!"

"Why? How can it affect them?" Mr. Bennet asked.

"My dear Mr. Bennet," she replied, "how can you be so annoying! You must realize I'm thinking of his marrying one of our daughters."

"Is that his purpose in coming to the area?"

"His purpose? No, of course not. But it's very likely that he'll fall in love with one of them. And I want him to see the girls as soon as possible, before our other neighbors introduce themselves. So you must visit him as soon as he arrives."

"I really don't see why I should," said Mr. Bennet. "You and the girls can visit him, or perhaps you should send them by themselves. Yes, that might be better, as you're as attractive as any of them, and Mr. Bingley might like you best."

"My dear, you flatter me," replied his wife, "I certainly have been called beautiful in the past, but I think a woman with five adult daughters should stop thinking of her own beauty. Mr. Bennet, I beg you to visit him. You know it's correct for the gentleman of the family to visit new neighbors first. I simply cannot take the girls to see him unless you have already met him."

"Surely you worry too much about the rules of polite society. I'm sure Mr. Bingley will be delighted to see you all. And I'll write him a few lines, which you can give him, agreeing gladly to his marrying any of the girls, although I must especially recommend my dear little Lizzy."

"Oh no, Mr. Bennet!" gasped Mrs. Bennet, horrified. "Please don't do that! And Lizzy is no better than the others, although I know she is your favorite."

"Our daughters are all very silly, ignorant girls, it's true. But at least Lizzy is a little more intelligent than her sisters."

"Mr. Bennet, how can you speak so unkindly of your own children? Oh dear, how ill I feel! Have you no pity for me? Don't you realize how I suffer?"

"Indeed, my dear, I've suffered *with* you for the last twenty-three years. But I think you will recover and live to see many more rich young men come into the neighborhood."

When he was young, Mr. Bennet had made the mistake of falling in love with a pretty but foolish young woman. During the long years of their marriage, he had had time to regret his mistake. He soon realized that his wife had little intelligence or common sense and was only interested in talking, shopping, and finding husbands for her daughters. His experience had made him rather bitter, and he could not stop himself mocking his wife, who never understood her husband's sense of humor.

So when, a week later, Mrs. Bennet discovered that her husband had in fact visited Mr. Bingley at Netherfield, she was surprised and very pleased. But she and her daughters tried in vain to persuade Mr. Bennet to describe the wealthy stranger, and in the end they had to rely on another neighbor's description.

"He sounds wonderful, Mama!" cried Lydia, the youngest and noisiest of the sisters. "Charlotte Lucas's father has been to see him and says he's quite young, very handsome, and extremely charming! And even better, he loves dancing! Everybody knows that means he's very likely to fall in love!"

As politeness required, Mr. Bingley came to visit Mr. Bennet a few days later. He was not, however, fortunate enough to see the Bennet girls, who were hiding behind the curtains in an upstairs room in order to catch sight of the handsome stranger. Mrs. Bennet planned to invite him to dinner, but in fact they met him at another social event first. The Bennets lived in the small Hertfordshire village of Longbourn, and public dances were regularly held in the nearest town, Meryton. The girls were greatly looking forward to this particular dance, because they had heard that Mr. Bingley would be attending, with a group of friends from London.

On the night of the dance, all eyes were on Mr. Bingley as he entered the room. He had brought his two sisters, with the husband of the elder, Mr. Hurst, and another young man, Mr. Darcy. Mr. Bingley was indeed good-looking and gentleman-like, and his sisters were fine, fashionable women. However, everybody was soon talking about Mr. Darcy, a tall, handsome man, who, it was said, had an income of ten thousand pounds a year. The ladies in the room gazed at him in admiration for about half the evening, until they became aware of his constant frown and his unwillingness to talk or dance. Then there was general agreement that he was proud and disagreeable, and considered himself superior to country people. Mr. Bingley, on the other hand, made himself popular with the ladies by dancing every dance and talking to everybody.

As there were not as many gentlemen as ladies, Elizabeth Bennet did not have a partner for one of the dances and was sitting watching the dancing. Mr. Darcy was standing near her, and when Mr. Bingley came up to speak to his friend, Elizabeth could not avoid hearing their conversation.

"Come, Darcy," said Bingley, "I hate to see you looking so cross! Why don't you dance with one of these lovely girls?"

"Certainly not," replied Darcy. "You know how I hate dancing with a partner I don't know. I would particularly dislike it at a village dance like this. Apart from your sisters, there isn't a woman in the room I would even consider dancing with. *You* are dancing with the only attractive girl here." He was looking at Mrs. Bennet's eldest daughter Jane, who was waiting for Bingley to join her for the next dance.

"Oh yes! She's the most beautiful creature I've ever seen! But just behind you is one of her sisters. She's very pretty, and I'm sure she's very pleasant. My partner could introduce you."

"Who do you mean?" And Darcy turned to look at Elizabeth for a moment. "No," he said coldly, "she's not attractive enough to tempt *me*. Go back to your partner, Bingley."

"No," Darcy said coldly, "she's not attractive enough to tempt me.*"*

This conversation did not endear Mr. Darcy to Elizabeth, but she told the story very cheerfully and amusingly to her friends.

The evening passed very happily for everybody else, and Mrs. Bennet was delighted with the effect her eldest daughter had had on Mr. Bingley.

"He danced with Jane *twice*!" she told her husband later. "He danced with all the others only once! And he really is so handsome! But his friend Mr. Darcy was so rude to poor Elizabeth! Luckily, she doesn't care! She wouldn't *want* to please him! Such a horrible, proud man! I simply hate him!"

When Jane and Elizabeth were alone, they discussed their dancing partners.

"I was really very flattered when Mr. Bingley asked me to dance a second time!" said Jane, blushing. "I didn't expect it at all!"

"Didn't you?" said Elizabeth. "I did. Dear Jane! You were five times prettier than any other woman in the room, but you're too modest ever to expect admiration."

"I have to admit that I liked Mr. Bingley," continued Jane in her gentle voice. "He's so good-mannered and agreeable!"

"He's also handsome," added her sister, "which makes his character quite perfect! But what did you think of his sisters?"

"Very pleasant when you get to know them. The younger, Miss Caroline Bingley, will be living at Netherfield with her brother. I'm sure we'll enjoy having her as a neighbor."

Elizabeth listened in silence. She was not convinced. "Jane is so kind!" she thought. "Always ready to see the good side of people's characters! *I* considered Mr. Bingley's sisters too proud, almost rude, in fact. I'm sure they feel superior to most other people, like Mr. Darcy." But she did not say any more.

After the dance the Bennet and Bingley families began to visit each other every few days. It became evident that Mr. Bingley admired Jane very much, and Elizabeth knew that her sister was close to falling in love with him. She was discussing this with her good friend, Charlotte Lucas, one day. Charlotte was a sensible, intelligent young woman of twenty-seven, the eldest daughter of Sir William and Lady Lucas, who were neighbors of the Bennet family.

"It's a good thing," said Elizabeth, "that if Jane *is* in love with Mr. Bingley, nobody will know, because she always behaves so cheerfully and normally."

"That's sometimes a mistake," replied Charlotte, shaking her head wisely. "If she doesn't show her feelings at all, even to the man she loves, she may lose the opportunity of catching him. Jane should use every moment she gets with Bingley to attract and encourage him."

"But I consider a man should try to *discover* a woman's feelings, not wait for her encouragement! And Jane probably doesn't know what her real feelings for Bingley are yet—she has only seen him a few times, not often enough to understand his character, or be sure that she really loves him."

"Well, I wish Jane success with all my heart," said Charlotte finally, "but I think she'd have as much chance of happiness if she married him tomorrow, as if she studied his character for a whole year. Happiness in marriage is simply a question of chance. I think it's better to know as little as possible about the person you're going to spend your life with."

Elizabeth laughed, sure that Charlotte did not mean what she was saying.

While observing Mr. Bingley's interest in Jane, however, Elizabeth had not noticed Mr. Darcy's interest in herself. Although at first he had not even considered her pretty, he now began to realize what a beautiful expression her dark eyes gave to her intelligent face and what an attractive figure she had. "Of course, she is only an unfashionable village girl," he told himself, "but her conversation is often quite amusing." Whenever they met, he did not speak to her, but stood near her, listening to her and watching her closely, conscious of a wish to know her better.

One evening at a party at the Lucases' house, Darcy was standing alone, as usual, away from the other guests, watching the dancing. His host, Sir William, came to speak to him.

"Mr. Darcy! Are you enjoying the dancing, sir? What a delightful entertainment it is!"

Darcy frowned. "Yes," he said with cool disdain, "it's something that any uneducated person can be good at."

"I'm sure you're good at dancing yourself, sir," replied Sir William cheerfully. "Look! Here's Miss Elizabeth Bennet." She was crossing the room at that moment. "Let me persuade you to dance with her. You cannot refuse to dance when so much beauty is in front of you."

"Indeed, sir," replied Elizabeth quickly, in some embarrassment, "I have no intention of dancing. You must excuse me."

"Miss Bennet, please allow me the pleasure of dancing with you," said Mr. Darcy politely, holding out his hand.

But with equal politeness Elizabeth refused again and turned away. Mr. Darcy was watching her walk away, with a slight smile on his face, when Caroline Bingley came up to him.

"Mr. Darcy," she said, "I'm sure I know what you're thinking—how boring all these silly little country people are!"

"Not at all, Miss Bingley. In fact, I was just thinking what pleasure a pair of fine eyes can give."

"Really! And who do these fine eyes belong to, may I ask?"

"Miss Elizabeth Bennet."

"Well! Let me be the first to congratulate you, Mr. Darcy! When will the wedding be?"

"Ah! That's what I expected you to say. A lady's imagination jumps from admiration, to love, to marriage, in a moment."

"Well, of course, when you're married, you will often have her charming mother and sisters to stay. How delightful for you!" And Miss Bingley, seeing that Darcy remained calm, continued to mock the Bennet family as amusingly as she could.

Jane's Illness

Mr. Bennet had a comfortable income of two thousand a year and a pleasant house in Longbourn. But, unfortunately for his daughters, after his death all his property would pass to a distant male relation. Mrs. Bennet's father had been a lawyer and had only left his daughter a small amount of money. She had a brother who owned shops in London, and she also had a sister, married to a Mr. Philips. He had been her father's clerk and now carried on his late employer's business.

Mr. and Mrs. Philips lived in Meryton, which was only a mile or so from the village of Longbourn. It was a most convenient distance for the Bennet girls, who were usually tempted there three or four times a week to visit their aunt or a dressmaker who lived opposite. The youngest daughters, Kitty and Lydia, were particularly regular visitors. Their minds were more vacant than their sisters', and if no better entertainment was available, a walk to Meryton always provided some amusement, as well as interesting local news from their aunt.

The latest news, which delighted Kitty and Lydia, was that the regiment which had recently arrived in Meryton was to stay there for the whole winter. The two girls now visited their aunt every day, and as Mr. Philips knew all the officers, Kitty and Lydia were soon introduced to them. At home they could talk of nothing but officers and their handsome uniforms: even Mr. Bingley's fortune now seemed hardly worth considering.

After listening to their praise of the officers one morning, Mr. Bennet said coolly, "From what I can see, you must be two of the silliest girls in the country. I've suspected it for some time, but now I'm convinced."

Kitty was embarrassed and did not reply, but Lydia, the youngest, continued to express her admiration for a certain Captain Carter, with perfect indifference.

"I am very surprised, my dear," said Mrs. Bennet, "that you should be so ready to think your own children silly. As it happens, they are all very clever."

"That is the only point, I think, on which we do not agree. I am afraid I must say that I consider our two youngest daughters unusually foolish."

"My dear Mr. Bennet, you mustn't expect such young girls to have the common sense of their father or mother. I remember when I used to like a red coat myself, and indeed I still do. If a good-looking officer with five or six thousand a year wanted to marry one of my girls, I wouldn't turn him down. And I thought Colonel Forster looked very handsome last night at Sir William's, in his regimental uniform."

Just then a servant entered with a note for Jane, which had come from Netherfield. Mrs. Bennet's eyes shone with pleasure, and she called out eagerly, while her daughter was reading it,

"Well, Jane, who is it from? What does he say? Tell us, tell us quickly, my love!"

"It's from Miss Bingley," said Jane. "She invites me to dinner at Netherfield, as she and her sister are alone. It seems her brother and the gentlemen are having dinner with the officers in Meryton."

"With the officers!" cried Lydia. "I wonder why aunt Philips didn't tell us that!"

"Having dinner in Meryton," repeated Mrs. Bennet, shaking her head. "That's very unlucky."

"May I take the carriage?" asked Jane.

"No, my dear, you'd better ride over there because it looks likely to rain, and then you'll have to stay the night."

"That would be a good plan," said Elizabeth to her mother, "if you were sure they wouldn't offer to send her home in *their* carriage."

"Oh, but they can't! The gentlemen must have taken Mr. Bingley's carriage to go to Meryton."

"I'd much rather go in the carriage," Jane said.

"But, my dear, your father can't spare the horses, I'm sure. They're needed on the farm, aren't they, Mr. Bennet?"

Mr. Bennet finally agreed that they were in fact being used that day in the fields. So Jane set out on her horse, while her mother called cheerfully after her, "I do hope it'll rain heavily, my love!" And Jane had not been gone for long before it rained hard. Elizabeth was a little worried about her sister, but Mrs. Bennet was delighted. "What a good idea of mine that was!" she said more than once, extremely pleased with herself.

Not until the next morning, however, did she realize the full extent of her success. After breakfast a servant from Netherfield arrived with a note from Jane to Elizabeth, explaining that Jane had caught cold on her wet ride and had been invited to stay at Netherfield until she recovered.

"Well, my dear," said Mr. Bennet, "if your daughter should become seriously ill and die, it would be a comfort to know that she died in a good cause and in obedience to your orders."

"Oh, I'm not afraid of her dying. People don't die of colds. She'll be looked after well at Netherfield. As long as she stays there, everything will be all right."

But Elizabeth felt really anxious and was determined to go to her sister. As the carriage was not available and she was not keen on riding, she decided to walk the four miles to Netherfield. Kitty and Lydia accompanied her as far as Meryton, where they went to visit one of the officers' wives. Elizabeth continued alone, crossing field after field and jumping impatiently over streams in her anxiety to see her sister.

When she arrived at Netherfield, with tired feet, muddy stockings, and a face healthily pink with exercise, she was shown straight into the sitting-room. The two sisters, Miss Bingley and Mrs. Hurst, could hardly believe that she had come so far alone and on foot in such bad weather, but they received her politely. Their brother, however, was more than polite: he was kind and considerate towards her. Mr. Darcy said very little, hesitating between admiration of her healthy good looks and doubt whether she should have come such a distance alone. Mr. Hurst said nothing at all, as he was thinking only of his breakfast.

Elizabeth was glad to be taken almost immediately to her sister's room, where she found Jane delighted to see her, but very feverish and unwell. The doctor came, and after examining his patient, he advised that she should stay in bed and take some medicine. Elizabeth stayed with her all day, looking after her, and the Bingley sisters also spent some time in the patient's room. However, in the afternoon, when it was time for Elizabeth to leave, Jane seemed so upset that Miss Bingley was obliged to invite Elizabeth to stay at Netherfield for the present, and a servant was sent to Longbourn to inform the Bennet family and bring back some clothes.

That evening Elizabeth went down to dinner, leaving Jane in bed in her room. She noticed the Bingley sisters' apparent concern for Jane change to indifference in a few moments and knew she had been right to dislike them at first sight. Mr. Bingley, indeed, was the only one of the group whose behavior she was satisfied with. His anxiety for Jane was evident, and his politeness towards herself most pleasing. But the others, she felt, treated her as an unwelcome guest. Miss Bingley was concentrating all her attention on Mr. Darcy, and Mrs. Hurst also joined in their conversation, while Mr. Hurst was only interested in eating, drinking, and playing cards.

When Elizabeth left the room after dinner to see if Jane needed anything, Miss Bingley at once began to criticize her.

"What bad manners she has! She's both proud and lacking in politeness to her superiors! She has no conversation, no elegance, and no beauty!"

Mrs. Hurst agreed and added, "She has no good qualities, except that she's an excellent walker. I'll never forget her appearance this morning. She really looked almost wild."

"She did indeed, Louisa. How silly of her to come at all! Why must she run around the countryside, just because her sister has a cold? Her hair looked *so* untidy! And her dress! Simply covered in mud!"

"I must say," said Bingley, "I didn't notice any of that. I thought she looked remarkably attractive when she arrived this morning."

"*You* observed her wild appearance, I'm sure, Mr. Darcy," said Miss Bingley, "and I imagine you wouldn't wish *your sister* to make such a show of herself."

"Certainly not."

"Walking four or five miles, whatever it was, up to her ankles in mud, and alone, quite alone! It seems to me to show a dreadful sort of independence, a country girl's indifference to what is acceptable."

"*I* think it shows a very pleasing affection for her sister," said Bingley.

"I'm afraid, Mr. Darcy," whispered Miss Bingley, "that this adventure has rather lessened your admiration of her fine eyes."

"Not at all," he replied. "They were brightened by the exercise."

After a short pause, Mrs. Hurst began again. "I have a great liking for Jane Bennet. She is really a very sweet girl, and I wish with all my heart she were well married. But with such a father and mother, and with such vulgar relations, I'm afraid there's no chance of it."

"I think the Bennet girls have an uncle who's a lawyer in Meryton."

"Yes, and they have another who owns shops in Cheapside! Such a *nice* part of London!" Both the sisters laughed.

"If they had enough uncles to *fill* Cheapside," cried Bingley, "it wouldn't make them any less charming!"

"But it must considerably lessen their chances of marrying men of any position in the world," replied Darcy.

Bingley did not answer, but his sisters agreed enthusiastically and continued mocking their dear friend's vulgar relations for some time.

Late in the evening, when Elizabeth was satisfied that Jane

was asleep, she felt she ought to go downstairs again. She found the party in the sitting-room, playing cards, but although they invited her to join in their game, she refused politely and picked up a book to read.

"I can fetch you more books to read, if you wish," offered Bingley, "but I'm afraid I haven't got a large library. Unlike you, I'm too lazy to spend much time reading."

"What a delightful library you have at Pemberley, Mr. Darcy!" said Miss Bingley. "And what a beautiful house it is! Charles, when you buy *your* house, I hope it will be even half as lovely as Pemberley."

"I hope so too," agreed Bingley.

"And your dear sister, Mr. Darcy? I expect she's grown since the spring. I want so much to see her again! I've never met anyone who delighted me so much! Such an appearance, such manners! And so extremely accomplished for her age!"

"I'm always surprised," said Bingley, "to find how very accomplished all young ladies are. How do they have the time and patience to learn all these skills?"

"Certainly people use the word 'accomplished' too loosely," said Darcy, "but I am far from agreeing with you about ladies in general. I cannot boast of knowing more than six who are really accomplished."

"Then," said Elizabeth, "your idea of an accomplished woman must include a great many qualities."

"Yes, a great many."

"Oh! Certainly," cried his faithful assistant, Miss Bingley, "an accomplished woman must have a thorough knowledge of music, singing, drawing, dancing, and modern languages, and besides this, a certain something in her manner of walking, in her voice, and in her behavior."

"All this she must possess," added Darcy, "and something more solid, the improvement of her mind by wide reading."

"I'm no longer surprised at your knowing only *six* accomplished women," said Elizabeth. "I rather wonder at your knowing *any*. I've never seen such elegance, intelligence, and knowledge, as you describe, in one woman."

Mrs. Hurst and Miss Bingley were both protesting loudly that they knew many women like this, when Mr. Hurst called their attention back to the card game. As this meant an end to the conversation, Elizabeth soon afterwards left the room.

"Miss Elizabeth Bennet," said Miss Bingley to Darcy, "is one of those women who try to appear attractive to men by undervaluing other women. *I* think that's a mean trick."

"It is true," said Darcy, "that there is meanness in *all* the tricks used by ladies to attract men."

Miss Bingley was not satisfied enough with this answer to continue the conversation.

The next morning Elizabeth was glad to be able to inform Mr. Bingley and his sisters that Jane was very much better.

In spite of this improvement, however, she asked for her mother to be sent for, as she wanted Mrs. Bennet's opinion of Jane's state of health. Soon after breakfast, therefore, Mrs. Bennet, accompanied by her two youngest daughters, reached Netherfield.

Elizabeth, although relieved to hear that her mother did not think Jane's illness serious, began to regret asking her to come, when she saw the Bingley sisters smiling at Mrs. Bennet's remarks. Elizabeth blushed for her mother, who could not help showing her lack of intelligence and common sense in everything she said.

Kitty and Lydia made an equally bad impression. They had

been whispering together, when suddenly Lydia, who was an attractive, confident, well-grown girl of fifteen, pushed herself rudely forward. She begged Mr. Bingley to hold a ball at Netherfield. With his usual politeness, Mr. Bingley promised he would, but Elizabeth saw his sisters exchanging meaningful glances. She was quite glad when her mother and sisters left. She and Jane were to stay another night at Netherfield, to allow Jane to recover completely.

That evening Elizabeth appeared again in the sitting-room. She could not avoid noticing how frequently Mr. Darcy's eyes were fixed on her, but as she felt sure that so great a man could not possibly admire her, she assumed that when he looked at her, he was criticizing her in some way. This thought did not cause her any pain, as she liked him too little to care for his approval.

In the conversations she had with him, she spoke in her usual slightly mocking manner, rather expecting to offend him, but was surprised by the quiet politeness of his replies. Darcy had never before been so charmed by any woman. He really believed that if she did not have such vulgar relations, he might be in danger of falling in love with her. Miss Bingley saw or suspected enough to be jealous, and her great anxiety for the recovery of her dear friend Jane was increased by her wish to get rid of Elizabeth.

Fortunately perhaps, for almost everyone at Netherfield, Elizabeth and her sister, who was now quite recovered, were returning home the next day. Only Mr. Bingley showed real sorrow at this and was concerned that Jane might not be fit enough to travel. Mr. Darcy was quite relieved and determined that no sign of admiration for Elizabeth should escape him now. Miss Bingley's politeness to Elizabeth, as well as her affection

Lydia begged Mr. Bingley to hold a ball at Netherfield.

for Jane, increased rapidly as the moment of departure approached, and she was able to say goodbye to them with many warm expressions of friendliness and a promise to visit them very soon.

Mr. Bennet was glad to welcome his eldest daughters home again, as he had felt their absence from the family circle, but

Mrs. Bennet, who had hoped they would stay much longer, was quite disappointed to see them come back in such a short time.

Mr. Collins Visits Longbourn

"I hope, my dear," said Mr. Bennet to his wife at breakfast the next morning, "that you have told the cook to send up a good dinner today as I am expecting a visitor."

"Who is it, my dear? I know of nobody who is coming, unless Charlotte Lucas happens to call in, and I hope *my* dinners are good enough for *her*."

"The person I'm talking about is a gentleman and a stranger."

Mrs. Bennet's eyes shone with excitement. "It's Mr. Bingley, I'm sure! Why, Jane, you never mentioned it! Well, I'll be extremely glad to see him. Lydia, my love, ring the bell. I must speak to the cook at once."

"It is *not* Mr. Bingley," said her husband. "It's a person whom I have never seen before."

This caused general astonishment, and he had the pleasure of being eagerly questioned by his wife and five daughters all at the same time. Having amused himself for some time with their curiosity, he finally explained. "I have recently received a letter from my cousin, Mr. Collins, who, as you know, will inherit all my property when I die and may throw you out of this house as soon as he wants."

"Oh, my dear!" cried his wife. "Please don't mention that hateful man. It's the hardest thing in the world to accept the fact that your property is not left to your own children, and I'm sure, if I were you, I'd have tried to do something about it."

Jane and Elizabeth tried to explain the legal situation to her again. They had often attempted to do this before. But it was a matter which Mrs. Bennet refused to understand, and she continued to complain bitterly about Mr. Collins.

"It certainly is most unjust," agreed Mr. Bennet, "and nothing can clear Mr. Collins from the guilt of inheriting this house. But if you listen while I read his letter to you, you may perhaps be a little softened by his manner of expressing himself."

He read aloud the following letter:

Dear Sir,

The disagreement between you and my late respected father always worried me, and since his death I have frequently wished to improve the relationship between our families. After a long period of study and training I have recently become a priest, and I have been fortunate enough to gain the patronage of Lady Catherine de Bourgh, widow of Sir Lewis de Bourgh. This generous lady has given me the post of rector at Hunsford, which was luckily vacant. Hunsford is the village near her own large country house in Kent. Here I carry out the duties of my profession whenever necessary, and I take great care to behave at all times with grateful respect towards her ladyship. As a priest, moreover, I feel it my duty to encourage all families in my area of influence to live peacefully. Because of this, I flatter myself that I am acting correctly in offering you my friendship. I am of course concerned that when I eventually inherit all your property, your daughters will doubtless be very poor, and I do apologize for this. I promise you I am ready to make amends in every possible way—but more about this later. If you do not object, I propose to visit you and your family on Monday November 18th, at four o'clock and shall probably stay until the following Saturday week. This will cause me no inconvenience at all, as Lady Catherine is far from objecting to my occasional absence from my duties.

I remain, dear sir, with respectful good wishes to your lady and your daughters, your friend, William Collins.

"So we can expect this peace-making gentleman at four o'clock today," said Mr. Bennet, as he folded up the letter. "He appears to be a most polite and serious young man. How considerate of Lady Catherine to allow him to visit us!"

"Well, if he is ready to make amends to the girls in some way, I shall certainly not discourage him," said Mrs. Bennet.

"Although it's difficult," said Jane, "to guess *how* he intends to do that, it's good of him to want to help us."

"*I* think he's peculiar," said Elizabeth. "He sounds too pleased with himself, and he speaks so politely of Lady Catherine! And why does he apologize for inheriting Father's property in future? We know it's not his fault. Can he be a sensible man, sir?" she added, turning to Mr. Bennet.

"No, my dear, I think not. I have great hopes of finding him quite the opposite. There is a mixture of servility and self-importance in his letter, which promises to be entertaining. I am impatient to see him."

Mary, the middle daughter, who spent most of her time reading and who seldom joined in family conversations, now remarked that in her opinion his letter was well expressed. But Kitty and Lydia did not show any interest in the letter or its writer. As it was highly unlikely that their cousin would arrive in a regimental uniform, they could not imagine having any pleasure in meeting him. Their mother, however, had changed her attitude towards Mr. Collins after his letter and was now preparing to meet him with such calmness that it astonished her husband and daughters.

Mr. Collins arrived punctually and was received with great politeness by the whole family. Mr. Bennet indeed said little, but the ladies were ready enough to talk, and Mr. Collins did not seem in need of encouragement. He was a tall, heavy-looking young man of twenty-five. His expression was serious, and his manners very formal. Soon after his arrival, he said to Mrs. Bennet, "Madam, I must compliment you on having such a fine family of daughters. I had heard much of their beauty, but I find them even more beautiful than reports have stated. I do not doubt you will see them all well married quite soon."

Mrs. Bennet never quarreled with compliments, and she answered, "You're very kind, sir, and indeed I do hope so, because otherwise they'll have nothing at all to live on."

"You refer perhaps to my inheriting the Bennet property?"

"Ah, yes, sir, I do! You must confess it is a sad business for my poor girls."

"I am very aware, madam, of the hardship to your lovely daughters—and could say more about this, but I am cautious of saying too much too soon. But I *would* like to say that I have come prepared to admire the young ladies. And perhaps when we know each other better—"

The bell rang for dinner, and the family moved into the dining-room with their guest. The girls smiled secretly at each other, as Mr. Collins praised the hall, the dining-room and all the furniture. Mrs. Bennet would normally have been delighted with such praise, but she could not help thinking that he was perhaps admiring it all as his future property. The dinner, too, he considered excellent, and he asked which of his charming cousins was responsible for it. But Mrs. Bennet explained quite sharply to him that they were very well able to afford a good cook, and that her daughters had nothing to do in the kitchen. He begged her pardon immediately for offending her and continued to apologize for about a quarter of an hour.

Mr. Bennet had hardly spoken up to now, but he thought it was time to enter the conversation. "You seem very fortunate in your patron, Mr. Collins," he said.

He could not have chosen a better opening remark. Mr. Collins spoke enthusiastically for several minutes in praise of Lady Catherine. "Never in my life have I witnessed such considerate behavior in a person of high birth! Although she is such a great lady, she has never treated me with disdain. She talks to me almost as an equal and gives me advice. For example, she has recommended that I marry as soon as possible. And do you know, she has asked me to dinner twice at her house! Some people consider her proud, but she has only ever been *kind* to me. She even took the trouble to visit my small house and was thoughtful enough to suggest one or two improvements—some shelves upstairs."

"That is very correct and polite, I'm sure," said Mrs. Bennet. "Does she live near you, sir?"

"Only a small country road separates my poor house from Rosings Park, her ladyship's home."

"I think you said she is a widow? Has she any family?"

"She has only one daughter, who will inherit Rosings and all Lady Catherine's property. A most charming young lady, unfortunately in weak health. I often pay her some little compliment on her appearance or her accomplishments when I visit Rosings. Lady Catherine appreciates these compliments to her daughter, and I see it as my duty to please her ladyship."

"I am sure you're right," said Mr. Bennet. "No doubt you are expert at flattering with delicacy. May I ask how you think of these pleasing compliments?"

"Some of them come to me at the time, but in my spare moments I do occasionally prepare a few words which may be suitable for different occasions."

Mr. Bennet listened to his cousin with the greatest enjoyment. Mr. Collins was as foolish as he had hoped. But by tea-time Mr. Bennet had had enough and, after tea, asked his guest to read aloud to the ladies. However, when a novel was handed to Mr. Collins, he looked shocked and protested that he never read novels. He chose a religious book instead and started reading in a slow, serious voice. Lydia could not hide her boredom for long, and after only three pages she interrupted him rudely, to ask her mother a question about one of the officers in Meryton. Mr. Collins was offended and refused to read any more although Mrs. Bennet and her other daughters apologized for Lydia's lack of manners.

Mr. Collins was not a sensible man, and neither education nor society had improved him. The respect he felt for his patron, and his very good opinion of himself and his new position, made him proud and servile at the same time. Now that he had a home and a considerable income, he had decided to marry. The Bennet girls, who would lose their inheritance because of him, had a reputation for being attractive and charming, and his idea of making amends to them was to marry one of them. He considered this an excellent plan and thought himself extremely generous and unselfish in carrying it out.

He had known he was right when he arrived at Longbourn and saw Jane Bennet's lovely face. As the eldest, she should marry first, and for the first evening *she* was his choice. But the next morning, after a fifteen-minute conversation with Mrs. Bennet, he had to change his mind. When he explained that he was hoping to find a wife among her daughters, she replied, with a happy smile, that her eldest daughter was very likely to be engaged soon. "But there are my other daughters, Mr. Collins," she continued, encouragingly.

Mr. Collins had only to change from Jane to Elizabeth, and it was soon done—done while Mrs. Bennet was pouring the tea. Next to Jane in birth and beauty, Elizabeth was the obvious choice.

Mrs. Bennet was delighted, hoping that she might soon have *two* daughters married. The man whom she had so disliked the day before was now a favorite with her.

Elizabeth Meets Mr. Wickham

When later that morning Lydia suggested walking to Meryton to see some of the officers, all her sisters except Mary agreed to accompany her. Even Mr. Collins went with them, encouraged by Mr. Bennet, who was by now most anxious to have some time to himself. During their walk, the girls listened politely to Mr. Collins' self-important speeches, but as soon as they entered Meryton, the younger ones no longer even pretended to be interested in his conversation, but looked eagerly around in search of the officers.

Just then all the young ladies noticed a very gentleman-like young man, whom they had never seen before, walking down the street with an officer they knew. They were all wondering who the handsome stranger could be when the officer came up to them to greet them. He asked permission to introduce his friend, whose name was Mr. Wickham, and who had apparently arrived recently from London to become an officer in the regiment. This was exactly as it should be, because the young man only needed an officer's uniform to become completely charming. He was very good-looking, with a very pleasant, sociable manner, and after the introductions, conversation flowed most enjoyably in the little group. They were still standing and talking happily together, when they heard the sound of horses and saw Darcy and Bingley riding down the street. The two gentlemen came straight towards the ladies to greet them. Bingley was clearly most interested in Jane Bennet and started talking particularly to her. Darcy, however, was just determining not to look at Elizabeth when he suddenly noticed the stranger. By chance Elizabeth saw Darcy's and Wickham's faces at the moment when they caught sight of each other, and she was astonished at the effect of the meeting. Both changed color, one white, the other red. After a few moments Mr. Wickham touched his hat, and Mr. Darcy nodded very slightly. What could this mean? It was impossible to imagine, and it was impossible not to wish to know.

In another moment Mr. Bingley, who did not seem to have noticed what had happened, said goodbye and rode away with Mr. Darcy. The two officers accompanied the young ladies to Mrs. Philips' house, but did not go in, in spite of Lydia's repeated invitations. Mrs. Philips was always glad to see her nieces, and she welcomed Mr. Collins most politely when he was introduced to her. She did not, however, have any more information for the girls about the agreeable Mr. Wickham.

"But I tell you what, my dears," she said brightly, "I'm giving a little supper party for some of the officers tomorrow. I'll ask Mr. Philips to visit Mr. Wickham and invite him to come too. Will you all come as well?"

The girls were delighted and agreed at once to this arrangement, and the whole group walked back to Longbourn, happily discussing the enjoyable evening they were going to have. Mr. Collins had been very impressed with Mrs. Philips' politeness, and when they reached Longbourn, he complimented Mrs. Bennet on her sister's elegance and charming manners.

The next evening the carriage took him and his five cousins to Meryton, and the girls had the pleasure of hearing, as they entered the hall, that Mr. Wickham had accepted their uncle's invitation and was at that moment in the house.

When Mr. Collins was shown into the sitting-room and had time to look around and admire it, he said immediately to Mrs. Philips, "Madam, I must compliment you on the size and furniture of this room. Really, I could almost imagine myself in the smaller summer breakfast-room at Rosings!"

This remark did not at first please his hostess very much, but when she heard from him what Rosings was, and who its owner was, and how much Lady Catherine's furniture cost, she realized what a great compliment it was. During the evening Mr. Collins found Mrs. Philips a kind and attentive listener, which was fortunate, as the Bennet girls could not bring themselves to listen to him any longer.

All the ladies were impatient to see Mr. Wickham, and when he came into the room, he appeared far more charming and gentlemanly than any of the officers present. He was the lucky man towards whom almost every female eye turned, and Elizabeth was the lucky woman beside whom he finally took his seat. His pleasant way of making conversation made her feel that he could talk interestingly about anything. As he did not play cards, which some of the party were doing, he stayed talking to Elizabeth for a large part of the evening. She hoped he would tell her how he knew Mr. Darcy, but she dared not mention that gentleman. Luckily, however, Mr. Wickham himself began to talk about it, although in a rather hesitating manner.

"Netherfield is quite near Meryton, I suppose? How long has—has Mr. Darcy been staying there?"

"He has been there about a month," replied Elizabeth. Unwilling to let the matter drop, she added, "He is a man of very large property in Derbyshire, I understand."

"Yes," replied Wickham, "his income is ten thousand a year at least. I know more about him than most people as I have been closely connected with his family since childhood."

Elizabeth could only look surprised.

"You might well be surprised, Miss Bennet, at my saying that, after noticing, as you probably did, the very cold manner of our meeting yesterday. Do you know Mr. Darcy well?"

"As well as I ever wish to!" cried Elizabeth. "I've spent four days in the same house as him, and I consider him very disagreeable."

"I've known him too long and too well to judge fairly whether he's disagreeable or not. But I believe most people would be astonished by your opinion."

"He is not at all liked here in Hertfordshire. Everybody is disgusted with his pride. You won't find him praised by anyone."

"I can't pretend to be sorry that he is valued as he deserves, but with *him* I believe it doesn't often happen. The world is blinded by his fortune and importance or frightened by his

Mr. Collins found Mrs. Philips a kind and attentive listener.

proud behavior and sees him only as he chooses to be seen." After a pause Wickham added, "I wonder if he's likely to stay at Netherfield much longer."

"I don't know at all, but I hope his presence won't stop you becoming an officer in the regiment here."

"Oh no! I won't be driven away by Mr. Darcy. If *he* wishes

to avoid seeing *me*, *he* must go. The reason I have for avoiding *him* is one I could easily make public to the whole world—he has treated me very badly. His late father, Miss Bennet, was one of the best men who ever lived and the most faithful friend I ever had. And whenever I'm with *this* Mr. Darcy, I think of his father with the most painful regret. Mr. Darcy has behaved wickedly towards me, but I could forgive him anything except the insult to his father's memory."

Elizabeth was fascinated and listened eagerly, but did not like to ask any questions. Mr. Wickham began to speak more generally about Meryton and the charming people he had met there.

"In fact, that's why I was tempted to join the regiment. I'd heard that Meryton society is most agreeable. Society, I confess, is necessary to me. I have been a disappointed man, you see. I did not intend to join the army at all. The Church ought to have been my profession, and I should at this moment have a comfortable income as a Derbyshire rector, if the gentleman we were speaking of just now had wished it."

"Indeed!"

"Yes—Mr. Darcy's father had always been very fond of me, and he intended to give me the post of rector of Pemberley. But unfortunately, after his death, when the post became vacant, it was given to someone else."

"No!" cried Elizabeth, horrified. "But how could that happen? Why didn't you get legal advice and claim what was rightfully yours?"

"Mr. Darcy's father had not stated his wish in writing. A man of honor could not have doubted his intention, but Mr. Darcy chose to treat it as a recommendation only. I really cannot accuse myself of having done anything to deserve to lose the post. The fact is, he hates me. I think he was jealous of his father's affection for me, which annoyed him from the beginning."

"This is very shocking! I hadn't thought Mr. Darcy as bad as this, although I've never liked him. I assumed he felt superior to everyone else, but did not suspect him of behaving in such a wicked, unjust, inhuman way!"

"We grew up together at Pemberley, you know. My father gave up all his time to take care of the Pemberley farms and was greatly appreciated as a close friend by the late Mr. Darcy, who promised just before my father's death to provide for me. The present Mr. Darcy did not choose to respect that promise."

"How strange that Mr. Darcy's pride has not made him help you! Surely he's too proud to wish to appear dishonest—which is what I must call him."

"He's certainly very proud—proud of his position, his family, his father, and his sister, too, you know."

"What sort of a girl is Miss Darcy?"

He shook his head. "It gives me pain to criticize a Darcy. But she's too much like her brother—very, very proud. She's a handsome girl of about fifteen or sixteen and, I understand, extremely accomplished."

"I am astonished at Mr. Darcy's close friendship with Mr. Bingley! How can Mr. Bingley, who seems so charming and kind, be friendly with such a man?"

"I don't know Mr. Bingley at all, but Mr. Darcy can be a pleasant companion if he thinks it worthwhile."

Just then they were joined by some of the others, and the conversation became more general. When Mr. Collins was talking to Mrs. Philips about his patron, Mr. Wickham looked quickly in his direction and then asked Elizabeth, "Does your cousin know Lady Catherine de Bourgh very well?"

"I don't think he has known her for long, but she has recently given him the post of rector of Hunsford."

"Perhaps you know that Lady Catherine is the present Mr. Darcy's aunt? I believe she is planning to marry her daughter, who will inherit a fortune, to Mr. Darcy."

This information made Elizabeth smile, as she thought of poor Miss Bingley's efforts to attract Mr. Darcy, which might all be in vain. The supper party came to an end, and Elizabeth went away with her head full of Mr. Wickham. She could think of nothing but him and what he had told her all the way home.

The next day she told Jane everything she had discussed with Mr. Wickham. Jane listened with astonishment and concern. She could not believe that Mr. Darcy could so little deserve Mr. Bingley's friendship, and yet she did not want to doubt the truthfulness of such an agreeable young man as Mr. Wickham. Elizabeth, however, felt sure that Mr. Darcy was to blame.

That morning an invitation arrived at Longbourn. Mr. Bingley had fixed the date for the ball he had promised to give at Netherfield, and it was to be on the following Tuesday. Every female in the Bennet family was looking forward to it, even Mary, who lifted her head from her book to say, unsmiling, "As long as I have my mornings free for serious reading, I do not mind meeting people in the evenings. I consider *some* relaxation and amusement is good for everybody."

Elizabeth felt so cheerful at the thought of dancing with Mr. Wickham that she made an unusual effort to speak kindly to Mr. Collins.

"Will you accept Mr. Bingley's invitation, sir? And if you do, will you, as a priest, consider it right to dance?"

"I shall certainly accept, and I am so far from objecting to dancing that I hope to have the honor of dancing with all my beautiful cousins. I take this opportunity of asking *you*, Miss Elizabeth, for the first two dances especially."

She was very surprised and rather annoyed. She had hoped that Wickham would ask her for those dances, but now she would have Mr. Collins instead! She could not refuse, however, and his request also worried her in another way. His manner to her seemed particularly flattering, which gave her the unwelcome idea that perhaps *she* had been chosen from among her sisters to be the rector of Hunsford's wife. As she observed the increasing number of compliments he paid to her beauty and character, she felt sure that he intended to propose marriage. For the moment, however, she decided to do nothing, but wait and see.

On Tuesday evening, when Elizabeth entered the hall at Netherfield and looked in vain for Mr. Wickham among the red coats gathered there, she was surprised and disappointed to see he was not present. She had never doubted he would come and had dressed with more than her usual care, looking forward to winning his heart, which she knew was already partly hers. But she immediately suspected that Darcy had persuaded Bingley not to invite Wickham, and although she discovered from one of the officers that in fact Wickham *had* been invited, but had been called away on business, she felt sure Wickham had wanted to avoid meeting Darcy, and she blamed Darcy for this. As a result, when Darcy greeted her, she was so annoyed with him that she could hardly reply politely.

But she soon became more cheerful and determined to enjoy the ball in spite of Wickham's absence. Unfortunately, the first two dances, with Mr. Collins, were painfully embarrassing, as her cousin had no idea how to dance and moved extremely awkwardly. She was relieved to leave him and have the third dance with an officer, who gave her great pleasure by talking about Wickham and his popularity in the regiment. After this, she was very surprised to be approached by Mr. Darcy and invited to dance. She was so astonished, in fact, that she accepted him without thinking and found herself standing opposite him on the dance floor. "What an honor for me, to be allowed to dance with Mr. Darcy!" she thought. They danced for some time in silence, and then she made a remark. He replied and was silent again. After a pause, she spoke again.

"Now *you* must say something, Mr. Darcy. You could remark on the size of the room or the number of couples."

He smiled. "I'll say whatever you wish me to say."

"Very well. That reply will do for the moment. Perhaps soon I'll observe that private balls are much pleasanter than public ones. But *now* we can be silent. Conversation needs to be arranged in this way so that those people who don't enjoy talking are not required to make any effort."

"Are you referring to yourself, or are you thinking of me?"

"Both," said Elizabeth, smiling, "because I think you and I are similar. We're both unsociable and unwilling to speak unless we can astonish and impress the whole room."

"I am sure you aren't like that," he answered. "I cannot say whether I am, or not. *You* obviously think so."

She said nothing.

"Do you and your sisters often go to Meryton?" he continued.

"We do," she replied, and, unable to resist the temptation, she added, "When you met us there last week, we had just been introduced to someone."

The effect was immediate. There was a new coldness in Darcy's expression. After a moment he said, with difficulty, "Mr. Wickham is so agreeable that he *makes* friends easily. Whether he can *keep* them is less certain."

"He has been unlucky enough to lose *your* friendship," replied Elizabeth sharply, "and in a way which will cause him hardship all his life." Darcy did not reply to this, and there was only time for a little more conversation before the dance ended.

Elizabeth went to find Jane and listened with delight as she described her feelings for Bingley and her confidence in his affection for her. But apart from Jane, it seemed to Elizabeth that if her family had made an agreement to appear as stupid as possible during the ball, they could not have been more successful. First Mr. Collins insisted on going to introduce himself to Mr. Darcy, the nephew of his respected patron, and was received very coldly. Then, during supper, Mrs. Bennet could not be prevented from talking very loudly to Lady Lucas about her great hopes of Jane's marriage to Bingley. Elizabeth blushed in embarrassment when she realized that the Bingley sisters and Mr. Darcy were able to hear. Finally, when some music was required, Mary Bennet went confidently to the piano and sang and played several songs, all rather badly.

The rest of the evening brought Elizabeth little amusement. She could not even go and talk to people she knew, as Mr. Collins seemed determined to stay close by her side all evening. Fortunately, her good friend Charlotte Lucas occasionally gave her some relief, by kindly listening to some of Mr. Collins' long speeches. At least Elizabeth did not have to talk to Mr. Darcy any more. He often stood near her, quite alone, but did not come close enough to speak.

At the end of the evening it was obvious to Elizabeth that although her family had greatly enjoyed the ball, the Bingley sisters were eager for these particular guests to leave. Mr. Collins, however, was enthusiastic in his praise of the Bingleys' hospitality, and Mrs. Bennet invited the whole Bingley family to visit Longbourn as soon as possible. She was feeling very satisfied, convinced that in three or four months Jane would be married to Bingley. She was also sure that Elizabeth would marry Mr. Collins. This was a good enough marriage for Elizabeth, who was her least favorite daughter, but not nearly as impressive as Jane's marriage to Bingley.

Mr. Collins Proposes Twice

At Longbourn the next day, soon after breakfast, Mr. Collins asked Mrs. Bennet for permission to speak privately to Elizabeth. Mrs. Bennet was delighted and hurried the other girls out of the room so that Elizabeth and Mr. Collins were left alone together. Elizabeth did not want to stay and got up to leave, but after a moment's thought, sat down again quietly, determined to listen and reply politely.

"My dear Miss Elizabeth," said Mr. Collins seriously, "this little unwillingness to hear me, this modesty of yours, can only add to your other charms. You can hardly doubt the purpose of my speech. Almost as soon as I entered the house, I chose you as the companion of my future life. But before I am carried away by my feelings, I think I should state my reasons for marrying."

Elizabeth was trying so hard not to laugh at the idea of Mr. Collins being carried away by his feelings that she was unable to reply.

"First," he continued, "it is right for a priest to marry, as an example to other people. Secondly, I'm sure marriage will add greatly to my happiness, and thirdly, which perhaps I should have mentioned earlier, my generous patron has advised me to marry. 'Find an active, useful sort of person,' she told me, 'a woman who can make a small income go a long way. Bring her to Hunsford as your wife, and I'll visit her.' So I decided to choose a wife from among my Bennet cousins, to lessen the loss to the family when the sad event of your father's death takes place. I flatter myself that you will appreciate my motives. And now, nothing remains but to convince you of the violence of my affection. I am quite indifferent to the fact that you bring little money with you into our marriage, and I promise you that I shall make no ungenerous reference to this after we are married."

It was absolutely necessary to interrupt him now.

"Sir, you forget I have given no answer. Accept my thanks for the compliment you are paying me, but it is impossible for me to accept your proposal."

"Of course I understand," said Mr. Collins, "that young ladies often do not accept a proposal of marriage the first time. I am therefore not at all discouraged and sincerely hope we shall be married soon."

"Sir," cried Elizabeth, "your hope is rather extraordinary after what I've said! I am perfectly serious. You could not make *me* happy, and I'm convinced I'm the last woman in the world who would make *you* happy. And I'm sure that if Lady Catherine knew me, she would find me poorly qualified for the situation."

"If I knew Lady Catherine thought so—" began Mr. Collins, looking very worried. "But I cannot imagine she would disapprove of you. And when I have the honor of seeing her again, I shall certainly tell her how modest, economical, and practical you are."

"Indeed, Mr. Collins, all praise of me will be unnecessary.

Pay me the compliment of believing what I say. I hope you will be very happy and very rich, but I cannot accept your proposal." She got up and was going to leave the room, but Mr. Collins was speaking to her again.

"I am far from accusing you of cruelty in refusing me, as I know it is the custom with elegant ladies in society to refuse a gentleman the first time. I hope to receive a more favorable answer next time I speak to you of marriage."

"Really, Mr. Collins," cried Elizabeth with some warmth, "you do puzzle me! I do not know how to express my refusal so that it convinces you!"

"You must allow me to flatter myself, dear cousin, that you do not intend to refuse me for long. My situation in life, my connections with the de Bourgh family, and my relationship to your own, all make my proposal a very suitable one. And you should remember that in spite of your many admirable qualities, it is not certain that you will receive any other offer of marriage, as you have very little money of your own."

"Sir, thank you again for the honor you have done me, but to accept your proposal is absolutely impossible. Can I speak plainer than that? Don't think of me as an elegant female, but as a thinking creature speaking the truth from her heart!"

"You are charming!" he cried, "and I'm sure that when both your excellent parents agree, you will accept my proposal!"

Elizabeth did not reply, but left the room silently, determined to ask her father, if necessary, to make her refusal clear to the self-deceiving Mr. Collins.

Mrs. Bennet had been waiting eagerly for the end of the interview, and when she saw Elizabeth leave the room, she hurried in to offer her congratulations to Mr. Collins. He received them with pleasure, adding that he was sure his cousin's refusal was a natural result of her modesty and delicacy of character.

"Refusal?" repeated Mrs. Bennet, shocked. "Lizzy refused you? Do not worry, Mr. Collins. I shall speak to her at once. She's a very obstinate, foolish girl, but I'll *make* her accept you."

"Pardon me, madam," cried Mr. Collins, "but if she's really obstinate and foolish, I do not think she would be a suitable wife for a man in my situation."

"Sir, you quite misunderstand me," said Mrs. Bennet, alarmed. "She's only obstinate in a matter like this. In everything else she is very agreeable. I'll see Mr. Bennet, and we'll arrange it with her, I'm sure."

She did not give him time to reply, but hurried to the library, where she knew she would find her husband.

"Oh, Mr. Bennet, we need you urgently! We're all in such confusion! You must come and make Lizzy marry Mr. Collins!"

Mr. Bennet raised his eyes from his book as she entered and stared at her with calm unconcern. "I do not have the pleasure of understanding you," he said. "What are you talking about?"

"Lizzy declares she won't have him, and if you don't hurry, he'll change his mind and not have *her*."

"So what should I do? It seems a hopeless business."

"Speak to her about it yourself. Tell her you insist on her marrying him."

"Call her in here. She shall hear my opinion."

Mrs. Bennet gladly rang the bell and the servant brought Elizabeth into the library.

"Come here, child," said her father as she appeared. "I've sent for you on a very important matter. I understand that Mr. Collins has made you an offer of marriage and you have refused?" When Elizabeth nodded, he continued, "Very well.

Now, your mother insists on your accepting. Isn't that right, Mrs. Bennet?"

"Yes, or I'll never see her again."

"You now have an unhappy choice to make, Elizabeth. From this day on, you must be a stranger to one of your parents. Your mother will never see you again if you do *not* marry Mr. Collins, and I will never see you again if you *do*."

Elizabeth could not help smiling, but Mrs. Bennet, who had been sure her husband supported her, was very disappointed.

"What do you mean, Mr. Bennet? You promised me you would *insist* on her marrying him."

"My dear," replied her husband, "I have two small requests to make. First, that you will accept that I know what I promised or did not promise, and secondly, that you will all leave me in peace as soon as possible."

That afternoon, Charlotte Lucas came to visit Elizabeth and found the family still in great confusion. The younger girls were quite excited by the news of Mr. Collins' proposal, and Mrs. Bennet was most annoyed with Elizabeth.

"Oh dear Miss Lucas," cried Mrs. Bennet, "can't *you* persuade Elizabeth to accept Mr. Collins? *Nobody* else wants to help me! Oh, how ill I feel! And look at Lizzy now! She's so unconcerned! But I tell you, Miss Lizzy, if you go on refusing every offer of marriage like this, you'll never get a husband at all! And I won't be able to provide for you when your father is dead, I warn you now. I told you in the library that I wouldn't speak to you again, and I won't. I have no pleasure in talking to an undutiful child like you. Not that I have much pleasure in talking to anybody, with my headaches. Nobody knows how I suffer! But of course those who do not complain are never pitied."

Her daughters listened in silence, aware that any attempt to calm her would only increase her annoyance. Elizabeth, however, was determined not to marry Mr. Collins, and in the end Mrs. Bennet was obliged to accept that fact. When Mr. Collins realized that Elizabeth had meant what she said, his manner towards her became coldly and stiffly polite. His long speeches and flattering compliments were transferred for the rest of the day to kind Charlotte Lucas, who took on herself the trouble of listening to him, for which all the Bennets were very grateful.

The next day a letter was delivered to Jane from Netherfield. Elizabeth saw her sister's expression change as she read it, and when they were alone, she asked about it.

"It's from Caroline Bingley," said Jane, "and it has surprised me very much. The whole party have left Netherfield and are on their way back to London, probably for the winter. They may not return to Netherfield at all. She says the only thing she sincerely regrets is leaving me behind in Hertfordshire, and she promises to write very frequently."

Elizabeth did not trust Miss Bingley's apparent affection for Jane. "I really don't think their departure matters very much," she said. "Mr. Bingley won't be kept in London by his sisters. I'm sure he'll be back at Netherfield soon."

"But perhaps he prefers to stay in London, where many of his friends are. But I haven't told you everything yet. Let me read you the part which particularly hurts me—"

Mr. Darcy is impatient to see his sister, and we confess we are also eager to see her again. Nobody is more beautiful, elegant or accomplished than Georgiana Darcy. Louisa and I have great affection for her and hope one day to call her sister. My brother admires her very much. He will have frequent opportunities of seeing her, and although I am his sister, I must say I think he is most capable of winning any woman's heart.

"What do you think of this, dear Lizzy? Isn't it clear enough? Caroline doesn't wish or expect *me* to become her sister-in-law; she's convinced of her brother's indifference towards me, and, perhaps because she suspects my feelings for him, she (most kindly!) warns me that he's very likely to marry someone else!"

"I have a totally different opinion. Miss Bingley sees her brother is in love with *you*, while *she* wants him to marry Miss Darcy. We aren't rich enough or grand enough for them, and she is eager to have a family connection with the Darcys, so that it may be easier for her to marry Mr. Darcy. So she follows her brother to London, hoping to keep him there, and tries to persuade you he doesn't care about you. But of course he's in love with you!"

"I really can't agree with you about Caroline. I think she's incapable of deceiving anyone. But Lizzy, my dear sister, even if she's wrong about her brother, and he *does* care for me, could I be happy in accepting a man whose sisters and friends all wish him to marry someone else?"

"You must decide for yourself, and if you consider it more important to do what his sisters want than to gain the happiness of being his wife, I certainly advise you to refuse him."

"How can you say that?" said Jane, smiling a little. "You know I wouldn't hesitate, although I'd be sad if they disapproved of me. But, oh dear, if he doesn't come back to Netherfield, I'll never have to make the decision!"

But Elizabeth was sure Mr. Bingley could not be kept away from Jane by his sisters and soon persuaded Jane to take a more hopeful view of the situation.

That day the Bennets, with Mr. Collins, went to dinner with the Lucas family at Lucas Lodge. Again it was Charlotte who spent most of the evening listening to Mr. Collins. Elizabeth was very relieved and thanked her friend gratefully for the trouble she was taking. But Charlotte's kindness had a particular aim, which Elizabeth was unaware of. Her plan was to encourage Mr. Collins to transfer his attentions to herself. In fact, she was managing so well that, when she said goodnight to him after dinner, she would have felt sure of success if he had been staying in Hertfordshire for another week. But she did not fully appreciate the fire and independence of his character, which caused him to get up very early the next morning and escape from Longbourn House, in a great hurry to reach Lucas Lodge and throw himself at her feet. She did not keep him waiting for an answer, and the happy couple found themselves engaged as quickly as Mr. Collins' long speeches would allow.

Charlotte's parents were delighted to agree to the marriage, and Lady Lucas began to work out, with more interest than she had ever felt before, how many more years Mr. Bennet was likely to live. Charlotte herself was quite satisfied. Mr. Collins, certainly, was neither sensible nor agreeable, but still he would be a husband. She did not think highly of men or of marriage, but she had always intended to marry. Although marriage might not always bring happiness, it was the only honorable way in which a well-educated woman with little income could provide a home for herself. Now twenty-seven, and lacking beauty, she felt she was lucky to have found a husband.

She knew, however, that Elizabeth, whose friendship she greatly valued, would be astonished and possibly disapproving. So she decided to go to Longbourn House to tell her friend the news herself. Elizabeth was indeed shocked at first and could not help crying out in surprise, but when Charlotte explained her reasons for accepting Mr. Collins, Elizabeth tried hard to understand. When the rest of the Bennet family heard the news, they were also astonished. Mrs. Bennet was quite horrified and could not stop complaining bitterly about Charlotte's wickedness, Mr. Collins' stupidity, and Elizabeth's obstinacy. Mr. Bennet was much calmer, only saying he was pleased to discover that Charlotte, whom he used to consider quite sensible, was as foolish as his wife and more foolish than his daughter!

That day was Mr. Collins' last at Longbourn, and he left with many speeches of thanks, as well as a promise to return very soon. Mr. Bennet warned him to be careful not to offend his patron by being absent from his duties too often, but Mr. Collins, although extremely grateful for this sign of Mr. Bennet's cousinly affection for him, was naturally eager to return to Hertfordshire to see his future wife.

Only two weeks later he did, in fact, come back to stay at Longbourn, but spent most of his time at Lucas Lodge, making arrangements for the wedding. Mrs. Bennet still felt very offended by him, but she was now becoming anxious about something even more important—Mr. Bingley's continued absence. Day after day had passed with no news since the arrival of Caroline Bingley's letter. Elizabeth was now rather worried, and Jane feared the worst. Finally a second letter arrived from Caroline Bingley, and when Jane read it, she realized that all hope was over. The Bingley family were staying in London for the whole winter, and Georgiana Darcy was a frequent member of their circle. Miss Bingley boasted joyfully of this friendship and looked forward to her brother's probable marriage to Miss Darcy.

Although she was deeply upset, Jane bravely tried to control

*When the rest of the Bennet family heard the news,
they were also astonished.*

her feelings. "Do not worry, Lizzy, I shall be able to forget him
in a while. I have nothing to complain of, as he made no
promises to me. I just thought he cared for me, but I was wrong.
Luckily, no one is hurt except myself."

"My dear Jane!" said Elizabeth. "You are too good. You

always think the best of everybody. Now *I* think the worst of most people and do not see much real value or common sense around me. Mr. Bingley, for example. He may not be intending to hurt you, but misery can be caused by someone being just weak and indecisive. I'm convinced his sisters and his friend, Mr. Darcy, are trying to influence him against you. Another example is Charlotte. I can't understand how she could agree to marry such a self-important, proud, silly man!"

"Dear Lizzy," said Jane, "we must respect Charlotte's decision. She may well be happy with Mr. Collins. And as for Mr. Bingley, we shouldn't expect a sociable young man to be so careful of his behavior. Women often imagine admiration means more than it really does."

"And men want that to happen."

"I prefer to believe that I was mistaken in thinking he cared for me and that his sisters love him and approve of his wish to marry Miss Darcy. I don't want to think badly of him or his sisters. That would be worse than anything."

Elizabeth had to accept Jane's wishes, and from then on, Mr. Bingley's name was seldom mentioned between them.

Elizabeth Visits Mr. and Mrs. Collins

The following Monday Mrs. Bennet had the pleasure of receiving her brother and his wife, who came as usual to spend Christmas at Longbourn. Mr. Gardiner was a sensible, gentleman-like man. The Netherfield ladies would have had difficulty in believing that a man who lived by buying and selling could be so well-mannered and agreeable. Mrs. Gardiner, who was several years younger than Mrs. Bennet and Mrs. Philips, was a pleasant, intelligent, elegant woman and a great favorite with her Longbourn nieces, especially the two eldest, who often stayed with her in London.

When Mrs. Gardiner had given the presents she had brought with her and described the newest fashions, she was obliged to listen to Mrs. Bennet's complaints.

"I've suffered greatly since your last visit, sister!" cried Mrs. Bennet. "Just imagine! *Two* of my daughters were very close to marriage—and then—nothing! I do not blame Jane, who would have got Mr. Bingley if she could, but Lizzy! Oh, sister! It is hard to think she might have been Mrs. Collins by now if she hadn't been so obstinate! The result is that Lady Lucas will have a daughter married before me. It makes me quite ill, to have such a disobedient daughter and such selfish neighbors. But your coming just now is a great comfort to me, and I am very glad to hear what you tell us about long sleeves."

Mrs. Gardiner made a suitably sympathetic reply to her sister-in-law, and later that day she found the opportunity to discuss the matter in more detail with Elizabeth, alone.

"I am sorry for Jane," she said kindly, "but, Lizzy, these things happen so often! A young man like Mr. Bingley frequently falls in love with a pretty girl, and when chance separates them, he forgets her very quickly."

"Yes, aunt," said Elizabeth, "but in this case it was not chance, but the young man's interfering friends, who separated Jane and Mr. Bingley. I'm sure he was violently in love with her."

"Poor Jane! She's so sensitive. I'm afraid she may not get over it for some time. Now, if it had been *you*, Lizzy, you would have recovered more quickly, by finding humor in the situation. But do you think I could persuade Jane to come back with us to London? Perhaps a change of air would make her feel better."

Elizabeth was extremely grateful to her aunt for this kind suggestion and felt sure Jane would gladly agree.

"I hope," added Mrs. Gardiner, "that she will not be influenced by the hope of seeing the young man. We live in such a different part of town that it is very unlikely they will meet unless he actually comes to see her."

"And that is quite impossible, because his friend Mr. Darcy would not allow him to visit so unfashionable an address!" But despite her protest, Elizabeth secretly thought that Jane *might* see Bingley in London and that a meeting would probably re-awaken his affection for her.

The Gardiners stayed at Longbourn for a week, and Mrs. Bennet made sure there was always some entertainment for her brother and sister-in-law. Whenever there was a dinner party at Longbourn House, some of the officers were always invited. Mrs. Gardiner, who had noticed that Mr. Wickham was a very frequent visitor and that Elizabeth spoke admiringly of him, took care to observe them both. She saw enough to make her a little anxious and decided to speak to Elizabeth about him when they were alone.

"Lizzy," she began, "I can see that you and Mr. Wickham like each other. But I must warn you not to get seriously involved with him. I admit he's a most interesting young man, but sadly he has no fortune. You are a sensible girl, and you must realize that you would disappoint your father by agreeing to marry a penniless young man."

"My dear aunt, do not worry. I'll take care of myself and Mr. Wickham too. He won't be in love with me if I can prevent it."

"Elizabeth, be serious."

"I'm sorry, aunt, I'll try again. At present I'm certainly not in love with him. But he is by far the most agreeable man I've ever met, and if he really loved me . . . But I would hate to disappoint my father or make any of you unhappy. I cannot promise what I will do, but I will really try to do what I think is wisest. I hope you are satisfied with that."

Her aunt replied that she was, and she received Elizabeth's thanks for her kind advice. Several days after this, the Gardiners returned to London, taking Jane with them.

The day of Mr. Collins' wedding soon arrived, and Mrs. Bennet had to watch Charlotte Lucas become Mrs. Collins. Before the bride left Longbourn for Hunsford, however, she asked Elizabeth to come and visit her in her new home as soon as possible. Elizabeth could not refuse, although she did not imagine it would be an enjoyable visit. It was arranged that Elizabeth would accompany Sir William Lucas and Maria, one of his other daughters, on their intended visit to Hunsford in March.

A week after Jane's departure, Elizabeth received a letter from her sister, saying that she had seen Miss Bingley and hoped to continue their friendship. Elizabeth shook her head over this. She was not surprised to hear from Jane a few weeks later that Caroline Bingley had made no further attempts to communicate with her former dear friend. Elizabeth was saddened to read of Jane's disappointment, but felt more cheerful when she told herself that Jane would no longer be deceived, by the sister at least. All expectation from the brother was now absolutely over. As a punishment for him, she seriously hoped he would soon marry Mr. Darcy's sister, who, according to Wickham, would make him quickly regret what he had thrown away.

At about this time, Elizabeth also received a letter from Mrs. Gardiner, asking about Wickham, and she was able to reply quite honestly that there was no danger of her marrying him. He had transferred his affections to a Miss King, who had recently inherited ten thousand pounds. Elizabeth saw exactly what was happening, but her heart had only been slightly touched, and she was able to convince herself that it was quite natural for such an agreeable young man to wish for fortune and independence.

January and February passed, and the time for Elizabeth's visit to Mr. and Mrs. Collins approached. She had improved the plan by arranging to spend a night in London at her uncle and aunt's house before continuing the journey into Kent. She was very much looking forward to seeing Jane, who was still staying with the Gardiners.

The journey seemed long to Elizabeth, because Sir William and Maria had nothing to say worth hearing. But when the coach arrived at the Gardiners' house at lunch-time, Elizabeth was delighted to see that her sister looked as healthy and lovely as before. In a private conversation with her aunt later, however, Elizabeth discovered that Jane had been suffering from periods of depression, although she always tried bravely to appear cheerful.

The afternoon and evening passed only too quickly, and the next day Elizabeth and the other travelers set off again. When the coach arrived in Hunsford, they were all quite excited to see, on one side of the road, Lady Catherine's great park, which they had heard so much about. At last, on the other side, they came to the Rectory, where they were warmly welcomed by Mr. Collins and Charlotte.

Elizabeth was more and more pleased she had come, when she found herself so affectionately received. She saw instantly that marriage had not changed her cousin's manners. He insisted on greeting them all with formal politeness and long speeches, and he showed them around the house, explaining its many good points in exhausting detail. Elizabeth could not help thinking that perhaps he was speaking particularly to her, as if wishing to make her feel what she had lost in refusing him. But although everything seemed neat and comfortable, she was unable to please him with a sigh of regret. In fact, she wondered how Charlotte could look so cheerful, with such a companion. But whenever Mr. Collins said anything of which his wife might be ashamed, which was quite often, Charlotte wisely did not appear to be listening. And when Mr. Collins showed them proudly around his garden, in which he himself enjoyed working, Elizabeth admired the serious way in which Charlotte praised gardening as a most healthy exercise and admitted encouraging her husband to work outdoors as much as possible.

Elizabeth had to confess to herself that, surprisingly, Charlotte really appeared to be happy. When Mr. Collins could be forgotten, the house seemed very pleasant and comfortable, and from Charlotte's evident enjoyment of her home, Elizabeth supposed he must often be forgotten.

The visitors had only been in the house for a day when a message came from Lady Catherine, inviting them all to dinner at Rosings Park the next day. Mr. Collins was delighted, and he congratulated his guests on their good luck. "I confess that I might have expected her ladyship to invite us all to drink tea at Rosings on Sunday," he said. "But to invite the whole party to dinner! So soon after your arrival, too! What a generous and considerate lady she is!"

The whole of the rest of that day and the next morning were spent discussing their visit to Rosings. This made Sir William and Maria quite nervous when the moment came to walk across the park and enter the great lady's house. Elizabeth, however, was unimpressed by what she had heard of Lady Catherine and remained calm.

She was interested to see that Lady Catherine was a tall, large woman, who held herself stiffly and proudly, and who received her guests with an air of disdain. She spoke loudly and decidedly on every matter and was clearly convinced of her superiority over other people. Her daughter, Anne, was completely different—a small, thin, ill-looking lady, who spoke very little, and only in a whisper.

The dinner was very good and was highly praised by Mr. Collins. His repeated compliments, which Elizabeth thought were embarrassing, appeared to please Lady Catherine very much. After dinner her ladyship talked continuously, giving her opinions without any fear of contradiction or even comment. She then asked Elizabeth many detailed questions about her education, her sisters, and her father's income. Although Elizabeth considered these questions extremely personal and almost rude, she answered them politely and calmly. At the end of the long evening, the visitors were driven home in Lady Catherine's carriage while Mr. Collins praised his patron for her elegance, intelligence, and hospitality.

This visit was repeated twice a week, but there was little other entertainment in Hunsford. Elizabeth had pleasant conversations with Charlotte, or read books, or walked along a narrow path by Lady Catherine's park, which no one else seemed to use. It was a quiet life, but she was satisfied with it.

However, two weeks after her arrival in Hunsford, she heard that some visitors were coming to stay at Rosings. Lady Catherine's nephew, Mr. Darcy, was expected soon, accompanied by his cousin, Colonel Fitzwilliam. The next day, the two gentlemen arrived and came almost immediately to the Rectory. Colonel Fitzwilliam was about thirty, not handsome, but very gentlemanly, and he talked pleasantly to the ladies. But Mr. Darcy looked as cold and proud as ever, and after greeting Mrs. Collins, spoke only a few stiffly polite words to Elizabeth. She took the opportunity of asking him if he had by any chance seen Jane in London recently and thought he looked a little confused when he answered that he had not had that pleasure. Soon after that, the two gentlemen returned to Rosings.

Colonel Fitzwilliam's manners were very much admired by the ladies, who felt that he would add considerably to the enjoyment of their evenings at Rosings. But it was not until Easter Day that they received an invitation from Lady Catherine, and when they arrived in her sitting-room, it was clear that she was far more interested in her nephews than in her other guests. Colonel Fitzwilliam, however, seemed really glad to see them, and he came at once to sit beside Elizabeth. They talked so agreeably and amusingly together that Mr. Darcy turned his eyes towards them and looked curiously at them several times. When her ladyship also noticed, she called loudly across the room, "Fitzwilliam, what are you talking about with Miss Bennet? Let me hear what it is."

"We're speaking of music, madam," he said, when no longer able to avoid a reply.

"Of music! Then please speak to all of us. I must have my share in the conversation, if you are speaking of music. There are few people in England, I suppose, who have more true enjoyment of music than myself, or a better natural taste. If I had ever learned to play, I would have been a great musician. But I often tell young ladies, practice is very important. I have told Miss Bennet several times that she will never play really well unless she practices more. And she is very welcome to come to Rosings and practice on the piano in the servants' hall. She won't be in anyone's way there, I can promise her."

Mr. Darcy looked a little ashamed of his aunt's insensitive words. Meanwhile, Colonel Fitzwilliam had persuaded Elizabeth to play some music, and she sat down at the piano. But when she had started playing, Mr. Darcy went to stand in front of the piano, where he had a good view of her face. At the end of her first piece of music, Elizabeth said, smiling, "You intend to frighten me, Mr. Darcy, by coming to listen to me? But I'm obstinate and won't be frightened."

"I don't think you really believe I intend to alarm you, and I've had the pleasure of knowing you long enough to be aware that you occasionally enjoy stating opinions which are not your own."

Elizabeth laughed at this picture of herself and said to Colonel Fitzwilliam, "Your cousin will teach you not to believe a word I say. Indeed, Mr. Darcy, it is very ungenerous of you to mention all my faults and perhaps rather foolish too, because I may take my revenge and tell things about you which your relations will be shocked to hear."

"I am not afraid of you," said Darcy, smiling.

"But let me hear your accusation," cried Colonel Fitzwilliam. "I'd like to hear how he behaves among strangers."

"Well, prepare yourself for something very dreadful. The first time I ever saw him was at a ball in Hertfordshire, and at this ball, what do you think he did? He danced only four dances! I'm sorry to cause you pain, but that is what happened. He danced only four dances, although gentlemen were scarce, and to my certain knowledge, more than one young lady was sitting down, waiting for a partner. Mr. Darcy, you must admit it."

"I had not at that time the honor of knowing anybody at the ball, apart from my own group of friends. I should perhaps have asked to be introduced, but I do not like to recommend myself to strangers. I do not find it easy to talk to people I don't know."

"You don't want to take the trouble to do it, Darcy, that's why!" said Colonel Fitzwilliam.

"I cannot play this piano as well as some other women," said Elizabeth, "but I've always assumed it is my own fault—because I don't take the trouble to practice. I know that I am *capable* of playing as well as anyone."

Darcy smiled and said, "You are perfectly right. You have spent your time in a much better way. No one who hears you could imagine any possible improvement. We neither of us perform to strangers."

Just then Lady Catherine interrupted them, to comment on Elizabeth's playing. "Miss Bennet would play quite well if she had a London teacher. Of course, Anne would have been a delightful performer if her health had allowed her to learn."

Elizabeth looked at Darcy to see his reaction to Anne de Bourgh's name, but neither at that moment nor at any other could she observe any sign of love or even interest in his cousin. Lady Catherine continued to give Miss Bennet advice on her playing, but at the request of the gentlemen, Elizabeth stayed at the piano for the rest of the evening.

Darcy Proposes Marriage

Elizabeth was sitting by herself the next morning, writing to Jane, while Mrs. Collins and Maria were shopping in the village. She heard the doorbell ring and knew that meant a visitor had arrived, but she was greatly surprised when Mr. Darcy, and Mr. Darcy only, was shown into the room.

He seemed astonished too, on finding her alone. "I apologize for disturbing you, Miss Bennet. I understood that all the ladies were at home."

"Please don't apologize, Mr. Darcy. I hope Lady Catherine and her daughter are well?"

"Very well, thank you." He said no more.

As he seemed in danger of sinking into total silence, Elizabeth had to think of something to say. She remarked, "How very suddenly you all left Netherfield last November, Mr. Darcy! I hope Mr. Bingley and his sisters were well when you left London?"

"Perfectly, thank you." That was all the answer he gave.

"I think I have heard that Mr. Bingley has not much idea of ever returning to Netherfield again?"

"It is probable that he will spend very little of his time there in future. He has many friends elsewhere."

Elizabeth did not want to talk any longer about Mr. Bingley, and, determined to leave the conversation to Mr. Darcy, she remained silent. He understood and soon began to speak again.

"Mr. Collins appears very fortunate in his choice of a wife."

"Yes, indeed. She is one of the few sensible women who would have accepted him, although I'm not sure I consider her marrying Mr. Collins as the wisest thing she ever did. She seems perfectly happy, however, and financially speaking, it's a good marriage."

"It must be very agreeable to her to be such a short distance from her own family and friends."

"A short distance, you say? It is nearly fifty miles!"

"And what is that? Little more than half a day's journey on a good road. Yes, I call it a *very* short distance."

"I would never have said Mrs. Collins lived *near* her family," cried Elizabeth.

"That shows how much you are attached to Hertfordshire. Anywhere outside the Longbourn area would, I suppose, seem far away to you." As he spoke, he smiled a little.

Perhaps he supposed she was thinking of Jane and Netherfield, thought Elizabeth, and she blushed. "Whether the distance seems long or short depends on many circumstances. If the family's income is large enough to pay for frequent journeys, then distance is not a problem. But Mr. and Mrs. Collins will not be able to afford to travel very often, despite their comfortable income. I'm certain my friend does not consider Hunsford *near* her family."

Mr. Darcy moved his chair a little towards her and said, "*You* cannot have a right to such a very strong local attachment. *You* haven't spent your whole life at Longbourn, I am sure."

Elizabeth looked surprised. Experiencing a change of feeling, the gentleman moved his chair away again, took a newspaper from the table, and, glancing at it, said in a colder voice, "Are you pleased with Kent?" They discussed Kent calmly and politely for a few minutes and were then interrupted by Charlotte and Maria, who had returned from the village. Mr. Darcy sat a little while longer, without saying much to anybody, and then went away.

"What can be the meaning of this!" said Charlotte, as soon as he had gone. "My dear Lizzy, he must be in love with you, or he would never have visited us in this familiar way."

But when Elizabeth described his silence, that did not seem likely, even to hopeful Charlotte, and they could only suppose that he had nothing better to do. In fact, from now on, both Mr. Darcy and Colonel Fitzwilliam called regularly at the Rectory. It was obvious that Colonel Fitzwilliam came because he enjoyed talking to the ladies, and Elizabeth was reminded by her own satisfaction in being with him, as well as by his evident admiration of her, of her former favorite, Wickham. But it was more difficult to understand why Mr. Darcy came. He did not often speak and seldom appeared interested in the conversation. Even Charlotte, who observed Mr. Darcy closely, was not sure whether he admired Elizabeth or not and began to hope that perhaps her friend might marry Colonel Fitzwilliam instead.

When she took her daily walk along the path bordering the park, Elizabeth met Mr. Darcy unexpectedly more than once. This was the more surprising because she was careful to inform him that it was her favorite walk so that he could avoid meeting her. It was also strange that, although he could just have greeted her and walked on, he always thought it necessary to turn back and walk with her. She could not quite understand him.

But one day, as she was walking, she met Colonel Fitzwilliam, not Mr. Darcy, and greeted him with a smile. They walked back to the Rectory together.

"Are you leaving Kent this Sunday?" she asked.

"Yes, if Darcy doesn't put it off again."

"He is fortunate to be able to arrange things as he likes."

"Well, we all want to do that," replied Colonel Fitzwilliam. "But he is used to doing what he likes because he is rich, and many others are poor. I, for example—I'm a younger son, you know, and won't inherit my father's fortune, so I shall never be rich or independent like Darcy."

"Now seriously, you cannot call yourself poor. When have you ever suffered because of lack of money?"

"Well, perhaps I haven't really suffered much yet. But there *are* difficulties. A younger son doesn't have a free choice when marrying. He cannot afford to marry a girl with no fortune."

Elizabeth blushed, thinking that he might mean her, and began to talk of something else. She asked him about Darcy's sister and mentioned that the Bingley sisters liked her very much.

"Bingley—yes, I know them. Their brother is very pleasant—a great friend of Darcy's," answered Colonel Fitzwilliam.

"Oh, yes, Mr. Darcy is extremely kind to Mr. Bingley and takes very good care of him," said Elizabeth drily.

"Yes, I believe Darcy *does* take care of Bingley. I'm thinking of a recent situation, which Darcy was telling me about on the journey here. He was congratulating himself on having saved a friend from a most foolish marriage. Of course, I'm not sure the friend was Bingley as Darcy didn't mention the name."

"Did Mr. Darcy give you his reasons for interfering?"

"I understood that there were some very strong objections to the lady."

Elizabeth could not speak for a moment. When she was able to control her anger, she changed the conversation. As soon as they reached the Rectory, she said goodbye to Colonel Fitzwilliam, and went straight upstairs to her room. At last she could think without interruption about what he had told her.

Bingley *must* have been the friend to whom Darcy was referring. She had always assumed that Darcy was involved in the plan to separate Jane and Bingley, but it now appeared that he, not Miss Bingley, was the main cause of all that Jane had suffered and still continued to suffer. The "very strong objections to the lady" probably consisted of having one uncle who was a country lawyer and another who was in business in London. There could be no possible objections to Jane herself as she was intelligent, beautiful, and charming. Nor could anyone object to Mr. Bennet as a father-in-law. When Elizabeth thought of her mother, she felt a little less confident. She was still convinced, however, that Mr. Darcy was interested in high-born connections rather than character or common sense. It was this, the worst kind of pride, which had destroyed for a while every hope of happiness for the most affectionate, generous heart in the world.

Thinking about all this made Elizabeth so upset and unhappy that she soon had a headache. It grew so much worse in the evening, and she was so unwilling to see Mr. Darcy, that she decided not to go to Rosings that evening with Mr. and Mrs. Collins. Instead, she stayed in the Rectory sitting-room, re-reading Jane's recent letters from London. She was saddened to discover that, although Jane never complained or referred to the past, in almost every line there was a lack of cheerfulness, which Elizabeth had not noticed the first time, and which now made her rather anxious. She was relieved to think that Darcy would be leaving Rosings in two days' time, and she herself would be with Jane in less than two weeks. Colonel Fitzwilliam would also be leaving with Darcy, but he had made it clear that he had no intention of proposing to her, so she did not intend to be unhappy about him.

Just then, she heard the doorbell and wondered if it might be Colonel Fitzwilliam, come to enquire about her health. But to her astonishment she saw Mr. Darcy walk into the room. In a hurried manner he began to ask how she was feeling. She answered him with cold politeness. He sat down for a few moments, and then, getting up, walked about the room. Elizabeth was surprised, but said nothing. After a silence of several minutes, he came towards her, with none of his usual calmness, and said, "In vain have I struggled. It is no good. I cannot conquer my feelings. You must allow me to tell you how warmly I admire and love you."

Elizabeth stared, blushed, doubted, and was silent. He considered this sufficient encouragement and confessed all that he felt, and had felt for a long time, for her. He expressed himself well, but it was not only of love that he spoke. He also talked of his pride and his sense of her social inferiority, which had made him struggle against his feelings for so long.

In spite of her dislike for him, Elizabeth appreciated what a compliment such a man's affection was, and she was at first sorry for the pain he was about to receive. But soon, as she heard his references to her inferior position, she lost all pity and became very angry. She waited patiently, however, until he had finished. He ended by describing the strength of his love for her, which, in spite of all his attempts, he had been unable to conquer with arguments of reason and common sense, and finally he asked for her hand in marriage. She could see that he had no doubt of a favorable answer, which only made her angrier.

"I believe society considers it correct, in cases like this," she replied, "to express grateful thanks. So if I could *feel* grateful, I would now thank you. But I cannot—I have never wanted your good opinion of me, and I cannot accept it. I'm sorry to hurt anyone, but it has not been done deliberately, and I hope the pain will not last long. The pride which, you tell me, has long prevented the expression of your affection, can have little difficulty in conquering your feelings after this explanation."

Mr. Darcy, whose eyes were fixed on her face, was both angry and surprised by her words. His face went pale, and he was clearly struggling to control himself. There was a dreadful pause, and then he spoke in a voice of forced calmness.

"And this is all the reply I am to have the honor of expecting! I might, perhaps, wish to be informed why, with so little attempt at politeness, I am rejected."

"I might as well ask why, with so evident a wish to offend and insult me, you chose to tell me that you loved me against your reason and even against your character. But even if my own feelings towards you had been favorable, do you think anything could tempt me to accept the man who has destroyed, perhaps for ever, the happiness of a most dear sister?"

As she said this, Mr. Darcy changed color, but he listened without trying to interrupt her as she continued.

"I have every reason in the world to think badly of you. Can you deny that you were the cause of Jane's separation from Mr. Bingley, and of her unhappiness? Can you deny it?"

"I have no wish to deny that I did everything I could to separate them and that I am delighted with my success. Towards my friend I have been kinder than to myself."

Elizabeth treated this last remark with disdain, but its meaning did not escape her. "But it is not only because of Jane that I dislike you. My opinion of you was decided long ago. I heard all about your character from Mr. Wickham. Now, what can you have to say on this matter? How can you defend yourself?"

"You take an eager interest in that gentleman," said Darcy, less calmly than before. The color was rising in his face.

"Who can help feeling an interest in him, when we hear of the unfortunate life he has had!"

"Unfortunate!" repeated Darcy contemptuously. "Yes, unfortunate indeed."

"And it was your fault," cried Elizabeth with energy. "You took away his chance of a comfortable income and a good position, which you knew had been intended for him. You have left him poor, dependent, and disappointed. You have done all this! And you can still treat the mention of his name with contempt."

"And this," cried Darcy, as he walked with quick steps across the room, "is your opinion of me! Thank you for explaining it so fully. But perhaps you might not have considered these offences of mine, if your pride had not been hurt by my honest confession of my reasons for not proposing to you earlier. Perhaps I should have hidden my struggles and flattered you by pretending I had every reason to love you. But I hate disguise of any sort. Nor am I ashamed of my feelings of pride, which are very natural. Could you expect me to delight in the inferiority of your family compared to mine?"

Elizabeth felt herself growing more angry every moment. "Mr. Darcy, you could not have made me the offer of your hand in any possible way that would have tempted me to accept it. The moment I first met you, I noticed your pride, your sense of superiority, and your selfish disdain for the feelings of others. Later events strengthened my dislike for you. You are the last man in the world whom I could ever be persuaded to marry."

"You have said quite enough, madam. I perfectly understand your feelings. Forgive me for having taken up so much of your

*"You are the last man in the world
whom I could ever be persuaded to marry."*

time, and accept my best wishes for your health and happiness."

With these words he hurried out of the room and the house. Elizabeth felt so weak that she sat down and cried for half an hour. She was so astonished to have received a proposal from Mr. Darcy! His affection for her must indeed have been strong to conquer all the objections he had to her family and position, objections which had made him prevent his friend marrying her sister. But his terrible pride, his shameless confession of what he had done to separate Jane and Bingley, and his cruelty towards Wickham soon removed any pity she might have felt for him.

Elizabeth Learns More about Darcy and Wickham

The next morning Elizabeth had still not recovered from the surprise of Darcy's proposal to her. Feeling in need of exercise and fresh air, she decided to have a walk. In order to avoid meeting Mr. Darcy, she kept away from her favorite path, but could not resist walking a little way into Lady Catherine's park. There she was astonished to see Darcy himself approaching her and calling her name.

"I have been walking some time in the hope of meeting you," he said. "Will you do me the honor of reading this letter?" And, handing her an envelope, he bowed slightly and walked quickly away. With no expectation of pleasure, but with the strongest curiosity, Elizabeth opened the letter and began to read it as she continued her walk alone.

Do not be alarmed, madam, that I shall repeat the offer which so disgusted you last night. I have no intention of mentioning again wishes which, for the happiness of both of us, cannot be too soon forgotten. I would not have written, but justice requires my character to be defended.

You accused me last night of two very different offences.

The first was that I had separated Mr. Bingley from your sister, in spite of their mutual affection, and the second was that I had destroyed Mr. Wickham's chance of future wealth and happiness in spite of my father's honorable promises to him. I hope that you will no longer blame me for either of these offences when you have read the explanation which follows. If I am forced to describe feelings which offend you, I can only say I am sorry.

I had not been long in Hertfordshire before I noticed that Bingley preferred your elder sister Jane to any other young woman. But I had often seen him in love before, and it wasn't until the Netherfield ball that I realized how serious his attachment was. I was careful to observe your sister closely, and as her manners and appearance were as pleasant and cheerful as ever, I remained convinced that she did not feel strongly about him. I was perhaps deceived by her calmness, and in that case, your anger has not been unreasonable. But I sincerely believed that her heart had not been touched. I objected to Bingley's possible marriage to her, not only for those reasons of social inferiority that I mentioned to you last night, but also for reasons which in my case I had tried to forget, but which I must state now. The behavior that evening of your mother, your three younger sisters, and occasionally even your father, was so lacking in social correctness that I made up my mind to save my friend from what I considered would be a most unhappy marriage. If you are upset by my description of your family's faults, it may comfort you to consider that you and your elder sister have avoided any share of blame and deserve nothing but honorable praise for your behavior. To continue—when I was in London, with the help of Bingley's sisters, who shared my opinion, I explained to him the disadvantages of marriage to your sister. This alone would not have been enough to prevent the marriage if I had not also been able to convince him of your sister's indifference to him. Then it was easy to persuade him not to return to Hertfordshire. I do regret one thing, however. Miss Bingley and I both knew that your sister was in London, but we hid the fact from Bingley. In this I consider I was less than honest, but I have no other apology to offer.

Your other, more serious accusation refers to Mr. Wickham. Here again I may cause you pain—only you can tell how much. In order to show you his real character I must explain the whole of his connection with my family. His late father worked for mine for many years, helping to look after the Pemberley farms. His son, George Wickham, received much kindness from my father, who paid for him to go to school and to university. My father hoped the young man would enter the Church. If he became a priest, I was to give him the post of rector in a village near Pemberley, when it became vacant. But even before my father died, I had discovered Wickham's weakness of character and lack of morals. After my father's death, Wickham wrote to inform me that he did not intend to enter the Church and asked for an amount of money instead of the post of rector. I knew that, with his character faults, he ought not to become a priest, and I therefore agreed at once. The business was soon arranged. He resigned all claim to the church post and accepted three thousand pounds instead. I hoped that I would not see him or hear from him again. But three years later he wrote again, this time to ask for the rector's post, informing me that his money had all gone and his situation was desperate. You will hardly blame me for refusing. Since then he has doubtless been violent in accusing me of injustice to all who will listen to him.

There is one more circumstance which I would like to forget myself, but which I must now mention. I rely on your keeping this confidential. A year ago, I sent my sister, who is ten years younger than I am, on holiday to Ramsgate in Kent, in the care of a female companion. Unfortunately, there was an understanding between this woman and Mr. Wickham, who also went to Ramsgate. With her help and encouragement, he spent a great deal of time with Georgiana and flattered her so much that she believed she was in love and agreed to elope with him. She was only fifteen at the time, and I am glad to say that she confessed everything to me immediately when I arrived unexpectedly in Ramsgate just before their planned elopement. Naturally, I dismissed the companion and wrote to Wickham, who left the place at once. He was doubtless most interested in my sister's fortune, which is thirty thousand pounds, but I cannot help supposing that he was also eager to revenge himself on me. I hope you will now clear me of all blame in this matter.

If, madam, you doubt the truthfulness of my description of these circumstances, I suggest you speak to Colonel Fitzwilliam. As my cousin and close friend, he knows every detail of these events and will be happy to support what I say.

I will only add, may God be with you.

Fitzwilliam Darcy

Elizabeth experienced a variety of emotions as she read the letter. She was astonished to discover that Darcy was capable of any sort of apology. It was with a strong prejudice against anything he might say that she began reading his explanation of what had happened at Netherfield, and at first she was too angry with him to treat him with justice. But when she went on to read his description of his relationship with Wickham, she hesitated. It was so very different from Wickham's story, which she would have preferred to believe. But after a few moments' thought she realized that Darcy's statement was much more likely to be true. She began to remember several things about Wickham which now appeared strange to her. On the first evening she had met him, he had told the whole story about his lost fortune and the Darcy family to *her*, a total stranger. Then he had boasted of having no fear of Darcy, but had avoided the Netherfield ball the very next week. In addition, he had waited until the Bingleys and Darcy had left Netherfield before making his accusations public. She reminded herself that no one in Hertfordshire knew anything about Wickham's past, so it was quite possible that he lacked morals, as Darcy said. She had to admit that Darcy himself, though horribly proud, had always shown himself to be a gentleman. Finally, Darcy would certainly not have dared to refer her to Colonel Fitzwilliam if he were not certain that his cousin could prove these statements.

She became absolutely ashamed of herself. "How badly I have behaved!" she cried. "How prejudiced I have been, I who have always been so proud of my ability to judge people! That pride has led me blindly into making a stupid mistake. Flattered by Wickham's interest and offended by Darcy's coolness, I have misjudged both of them. Till this moment, I never knew myself."

She re-read what Darcy had to say about Jane, and this time was forced to admit that Jane had displayed few outward signs of her feelings for Bingley. Charlotte had even commented on it. Then when Elizabeth looked again at Darcy's comments on her family's behavior, her sense of shame was very great, and she could not deny the justice of his words. Feeling more miserable than she had ever felt before, she slowly returned to the Rectory, where she had difficulty in maintaining a cheerful appearance.

Mr. Darcy and Colonel Fitzwilliam left Rosings the next day and were sadly missed by their aunt, who now had so little entertainment that she invited the Collinses and their visitors several times that week. As Elizabeth only had a few days left before the end of her visit, she thought it fortunate that most of her time was occupied. When she had a moment to herself, it was a great relief to walk outside in the garden or the park, alone with her thoughts. She soon knew Mr. Darcy's letter by heart. Although she was still angry with him for the proud, over-confident way in which he had proposed, her anger turned against herself when she considered how unjustly she had criticized and accused him. She respected his character and felt pity for his disappointment, but did not for a moment regret her refusal, or have the slightest desire to see him ever again.

She was saddened when she thought of her family. Her father enjoyed laughing at Kitty's and Lydia's foolishness so much that he never attempted to control his two youngest daughters, and her mother, whose own behavior was far from correct, was completely unaware that anything was wrong. And poor Jane! It now appeared that Bingley's affection had been sincere, and Jane's disappointment had been indirectly caused by the behavior of her own near relations.

On Saturday morning Elizabeth said goodbye to her friend Charlotte, feeling sorry to leave her with such a husband. But Charlotte, although regretting the departure of her visitors, appeared quite content with her domestic arrangements. Mr. Collins took care to say to Elizabeth, before she left, "I do hope, my dear Miss Elizabeth, that you will be as happy in marriage as I am. My dear Charlotte and I have one mind and one way of thinking. We seem to be *made* for each other."

"It is most fortunate when that is the case," was all that Elizabeth could safely reply.

By midday she had arrived in London, where she had arranged to stay a few days at her aunt's house. There was, however, no opportunity to discuss Mr. Darcy's letter with Jane until they both reached Longbourn again, at the end of the week.

It was pleasant to be at home again, but Elizabeth was very conscious of her younger sisters' silliness. They were full of the sad news they had just heard, that the regiment was leaving Meryton in two weeks' time and would be staying for the summer in Brighton, a holiday town on the south coast. Lydia and her mother were trying hard to persuade Mr. Bennet to take them to Brighton too, for several months, as the summer would be so miserable in Hertfordshire without the officers. Fortunately, Elizabeth felt sure her father would not agree to this foolish idea.

When she and Jane were alone, she told her sister about Darcy's proposal of marriage. Jane was astonished, but soon her sisterly feelings made her think it quite natural, and her kind heart felt pity for Darcy's disappointment. However, when she heard about George Wickham's wickedness, as explained in Darcy's letter, she was deeply shocked. After some discussion, the sisters decided not to tell anyone what they knew about Wickham, as he would soon be leaving Meryton in any case.

Elizabeth felt greatly relieved by this conversation. She had got rid of two of her secrets and was certain of a willing listener in Jane, whenever she might wish to talk again of either. But she dared not tell the third and explain to Jane how sincere Bingley's feelings for her had been. She could see that Jane was not happy because of her continued warm affection for Bingley. However, there seemed little chance of Bingley marrying her now, and Elizabeth did not want to deepen Jane's feelings of regret for her lost happiness.

Elizabeth in Derbyshire

During the week before the regiment's departure, all the young ladies in the Meryton area became extremely depressed. Only the two elder Miss Bennets were still able to eat, drink, sleep, and lead a normal life. They were often scolded by Kitty and Lydia, who could not understand such hard-heartedness.

"How shall we manage without the officers!" they cried miserably. "How *can* you smile like that, Lizzy?"

Their affectionate mother shared all their sadness. "I remember when Colonel Millar's regiment went away, twenty-five years ago," she said, "I thought my heart was broken."

"I'm sure *mine* will be broken," said Lydia.

"If we could only go to Brighton!" said Mrs. Bennet. "I'm certain a little sea-bathing would be good for me."

"Oh yes! But Papa is *so* disagreeable about it."

Elizabeth tried not to listen, but could not help seeing the justice of Darcy's objections to her family.

But soon Lydia's bitterness changed to absolute delight when she received an invitation from Colonel Forster's wife to accompany her to Brighton with the regiment. Mrs. Forster was a very young woman, only recently married, and as cheerful and sociable as Lydia, with whom she had been friendly for two months. Poor Kitty was very upset at not being included in the invitation, but Lydia cared nothing for her sister's feelings. She ran wildly through the house, calling for everyone's congratulations, and laughing and talking more loudly than ever.

Elizabeth could not share her sister's happiness and felt it was her duty to advise her father secretly to refuse permission for Lydia to go. But she could not convince him that Lydia would be in any real danger, and so all the arrangements were made for her sister's departure. Elizabeth thought her father was wrong, however, and was still worried about how Lydia would behave in an atmosphere of greater freedom and among the temptations of a fashionable seaside town like Brighton.

Elizabeth had seen Mr. Wickham regularly since her return from Kent at family parties and visits. She no longer thought him so agreeable. As the rich Miss King had left Meryton to stay with her uncle, Mr. Wickham appeared eager to transfer his affections back to Elizabeth. His confidence in his own charm and ability to please annoyed Elizabeth very much, so that when she met him for the last time before the regiment's departure, she spoke quite coldly to him. In reply to a polite question of his about her Hunsford visit, she could not stop herself mentioning her frequent meetings with Mr. Darcy and her favorable opinion of that gentleman's character. Wickham looked a little embarrassed and made no further attempt to charm Elizabeth. They separated at last with mutual politeness and possibly a mutual desire never to meet again.

When Lydia left for Brighton, Elizabeth had to put up with Mrs. Bennet's and Kitty's constant complaints that Longbourn had become very dull. Fortunately, she was able to look forward to a trip which she would soon be taking with Mr. and Mrs. Gardiner. They had planned to visit the Lake District, but Mrs. Gardiner had recently written to say that as her husband's business made it necessary to shorten their holiday to three weeks, they would not have time to visit the whole of the Lake District comfortably. Instead, she suggested visiting Derbyshire, an area with a particularly strong attraction for her, as she had spent a large part of her early life there. Elizabeth was disappointed, but accepted the new plan at once. Although it was impossible to hear of Derbyshire without thinking of Pemberley and its owner, she felt sure she could avoid meeting Mr. Darcy there.

Four weeks later, Mr. and Mrs. Gardiner arrived at Longbourn, where they had arranged to leave their children in Jane's care. The next day they set out with Elizabeth on their journey. The three of them made excellent traveling companions, sharing an intelligent interest in the people and places they saw on their way and a strong affection for each other. After visiting Oxford, Blenheim, Warwick, Kenilworth, and Birmingham, they arrived in Derbyshire and decided to stay in the small town of Lambton, where Mrs. Gardiner had lived before her marriage. Elizabeth discovered that Mr. Darcy's house, Pemberley, was only five miles away from Lambton.

"I often used to go to Pemberley when I was younger," said Mrs. Gardiner. "Wouldn't you like to see it, Lizzy? We could go tomorrow. It's a beautiful place. Wickham spent his youth there, you know."

"I—I am rather tired of large country houses, aunt," said Elizabeth, forced to pretend. How dreadful it would be to meet Mr. Darcy while viewing his house! But when she asked a servant at the hotel one or two careful questions that evening, she was told that Mr. Darcy was not at home at the moment. Greatly relieved, she felt able to agree to her aunt's suggestion, when it was repeated the next morning, and Mr. Gardiner ordered a carriage immediately.

In a short time they entered the gates of Pemberley park and drove through an extensive and beautiful wood. At the top of a hill they had their first view of Pemberley House, situated on the other side of a valley, with a line of high, wooded hills behind. The house was a large, handsome, stone building, which appeared to fit naturally into the scenery. Mr. and Mrs. Gardiner were warm in their admiration, and Elizabeth was delighted. At that moment she felt that to be mistress of Pemberley might be worthwhile!

They drove up to the front door and asked to be allowed to visit the house. The Pemberley housekeeper, a respectable, elderly woman, showed them around. All the rooms were of a good size and elegantly yet sensibly furnished. From every window there was an attractive view. Elizabeth began to admire the owner's taste in everything she saw.

"And I might have been mistress of this place!" she thought. "Instead of viewing these rooms as a stranger, I might be welcoming my uncle and aunt as visitors. But no," she suddenly remembered, "that could never be. I wouldn't have been able to invite my uncle and aunt, or any other of my vulgar family connections." This was a lucky thought, which saved her from something like regret.

She longed to enquire of the housekeeper whether her master were really absent, but luckily her uncle asked the question instead. It was quite alarming to hear that Mr. Darcy was expected to arrive the next day, with a large group of friends.

How glad Elizabeth was that their own journey had not been delayed a day!

Mr. and Mrs. Gardiner were enjoying their conversation with the housekeeper, who seemed content to talk about her master.

"Mr. Darcy is a very handsome gentleman, as you will see from the painting upstairs. His sister is most attractive too, and so accomplished! She plays and sings the whole day. My master has just sent a new piano from London for her. He's such a kind brother—he'll do anything for Miss Georgiana."

"Does Mr. Darcy spend much time at Pemberley?" asked Mr. Gardiner.

"Not as much as I'd like, sir."

"If your master married, he might spend more time here!"

"Yes, sir, but I don't know when that'll be. I don't know who is good enough for him." Mr. and Mrs. Gardiner smiled, and Elizabeth listened with increasing astonishment as the housekeeper continued. "It's no more than the truth. Everybody who knows him says the same. He's never spoken a cross word to me, and I've known him since he was a baby. Some people call him proud, but I've never seen any of that. He's the best master that ever lived."

Elizabeth almost stared at her. "Can this be Mr. Darcy?" she wondered. This was the most extraordinary praise for the man she had always thought so disagreeable and proud, especially with people he considered inferior to himself. She longed to hear more, but now the housekeeper was leading them upstairs. Soon Elizabeth found herself in front of the painting of Mr. Darcy. He was smiling at her, just as she remembered him smiling sometimes when he looked at her. She looked at the picture silently for several minutes before going downstairs with the others. At that moment Elizabeth certainly felt more warmly towards Mr. Darcy than at any time since their first meeting. She was beginning to realize that she had underestimated his character. His housekeeper's opinion of him was totally favorable, and what praise is more valuable than the praise of an intelligent servant? As she stood in front of his picture, she gratefully remembered the warmth of his feelings for her, and she began to forget the way in which he had expressed them.

As they had now seen all the rooms which were open to the public, the housekeeper called the gardener, who was going to show them the park and gardens. They were just walking away from the house, when Elizabeth turned to have one last look and saw the owner of Pemberley come suddenly forward from behind the house.

They were within twenty yards of each other, and Elizabeth could not avoid his seeing her. Their eyes instantly met, and they both blushed. He appeared very surprised, but, recovering quickly, approached and spoke to Elizabeth, if not calmly, at least with perfect politeness. Astonished and confused, she received his greetings with embarrassment. Soon he could find no more to say and left her to return to the house. Mr. and Mrs. Gardiner, who had been watching from a distance, expressed their admiration of his appearance, but Elizabeth could only think of her feelings. How unfortunate that she had come! She blushed again. It might seem as if she had planned this meeting with him. And his behavior was so different! Never before had she heard him speak so politely and so gently. What could it mean?

Her head full of these thoughts, she joined her uncle and aunt in their walk through the gardens. They were walking slowly beside an attractive stream when they noticed Mr. Darcy coming towards them. This time Elizabeth was able to control

Elizabeth turned, and saw the owner of Pemberley come suddenly forward.

herself better, and she returned his greetings politely. She hid a smile when he asked her to do him the honor of introducing him to her friends, as she felt sure he was not expecting the well-mannered Gardiners to be some of her low-born relations. He certainly seemed surprised when she introduced her uncle and aunt, but took care to talk for some time to Mr. Gardiner, with every appearance of interest. Elizabeth was delighted that these relations, at least, could not be criticized for their poor behavior or lack of intelligence. On their way back to the house, Mr. Darcy walked beside Elizabeth. There was a short silence before she spoke.

"Your housekeeper informed us you would not arrive until tomorrow, so I had not expected to find you here."

"It is true. I came early on business. The rest of the party will be here tomorrow. Among them are Mr. Bingley and his sisters, whom you know." He continued after a pause, "And there is one other person who particularly wishes to meet you. Will you allow me, or do I ask too much, to introduce my sister to you?"

Surprised but flattered by this great compliment, Elizabeth gave her permission. When they arrived at the house, Mr. Darcy offered them some refreshment, but they politely refused. Mr. Darcy helped the ladies into the carriage, and as it drove away from Pemberley, Elizabeth watched him walking slowly back towards the house. Mr. and Mrs. Gardiner were loud in their praise of him, but Elizabeth said very little.

The very next morning Mr. Darcy brought his sister to visit Elizabeth and the Gardiners at the hotel in Lambton. Mr. and Mrs. Gardiner were astonished by the honor they were receiving, but Elizabeth's obvious embarrassment and Darcy's haste in making the visit so immediately, soon provided them with an explanation. They observed their niece and Darcy carefully during the visit and could not doubt that the gentleman was in love, although they were not certain of the lady's feelings.

Elizabeth was delighted to discover that Georgiana Darcy, far from being proud, as Wickham had said, was just very shy, with quiet, gentle manners. It was clear that she greatly admired her brother and had every intention of liking Miss Bennet as Darcy had spoken of her so favorably. Elizabeth was also satisfied to see that Bingley, who was with the Darcys, did not seem particularly interested in Georgiana, in spite of Caroline Bingley's wishes. And she had to admit that she had never seen Mr. Darcy behaving so sociably and pleasantly, not only to herself, but also to the relations to whom he had referred with such disdain during that last conversation in Hunsford Rectory. Elizabeth herself was more than usually anxious to make herself agreeable to everybody, and she succeeded because Bingley was ready, Georgiana was eager, and Darcy determined, to be pleased.

Miss Darcy, encouraged by her brother, invited Elizabeth and the Gardiners to dinner at Pemberley in two days' time, and when this invitation had been accepted, the Darcys and Mr. Bingley left, with many warm expressions of politeness on both sides. Mr. and Mrs. Gardiner were very curious about their niece's feelings for Mr. Darcy, but were careful not to question her.

That evening Elizabeth lay awake for two whole hours, trying to understand how she felt about him. She now thought of him with respect and a certain admiration, and she was deeply grateful to him, not only for having once loved her, but for still loving her enough to forgive her bitter rejection of him as well as all her unjust accusations. The change she had noticed, in a man who was once so proud, must be caused by his love for her. Now, since she was almost sure that if she wanted, she could encourage him to propose to her again, she only had to decide how far she wished to be involved in his future happiness, in which she already felt a real interest.

10

Lydia and Wickham

On the third morning of her visit to Lambton, Elizabeth received two letters from Jane. The first had been badly addressed and sent elsewhere, then redirected. Her aunt and uncle were out walking, so she sat down to read them at once. The first had been written five days before and started just as expected, with a description of Longbourn dinner parties and visits, but the second half of this letter was dated a day later and was evidently written in a great hurry. This is what it said:

Since writing the above, dear Lizzy, something most unexpected and serious has happened. But I do not wish to alarm you, we are all well. It concerns poor Lydia. An express letter came at midnight last night, when we were all in bed, from Colonel Forster, to inform us that she had run away to Scotland with one of his officers, with Wickham in fact! There, of course, she can marry without her parents' approval. Imagine our surprise. What a foolish marriage for both of them! But at least he is not interested in her money, as he must know my father can give her almost nothing. Kitty admits that she knew about Lydia's attachment to Wickham, from Lydia's letters. Our poor mother is very upset. I must finish now, as I cannot stay away from her for long. I hope you can read this. I hardly know what I have written.

Without allowing herself time to think, Elizabeth opened the second letter, dated a day later, and read impatiently:

My dearest sister,

I am so confused I cannot write properly. I have bad news for you. Foolish though a marriage between Mr. Wickham and our poor Lydia might be, we are now only too anxious to hear that it has taken place. There is reason to fear they have not gone to Scotland. Colonel Forster arrived here yesterday. He tells us that one of the officers, a close friend of Wickham, believes that Wickham never intended to go to Scotland, or to marry Lydia at all. The colonel followed the couple as far as London, but they have not been seen leaving the capital. Our anxiety, my dear Lizzy, is very great. My father and mother believe the worst, and the colonel fears Wickham is not a man to be trusted, but I cannot believe him to be so wicked. And is Lydia so completely lacking in morals, that she could live with a man without being married? Impossible. Now my poor mother is really ill, my father is angry, for perhaps the first time in his life, and Kitty is being scolded for keeping the attachment a secret. While I am glad, dearest Lizzy, that you have been spared some of the confusion and worry we have been experiencing, I cannot help begging you all to come home as soon as possible. My father is going to London with the colonel to try to find Lydia. I think he is too upset to achieve results in the best and safest way, and my uncle's advice and help would be everything in the world. I rely on his goodness.

"Oh! Where, where is my uncle?" cried Elizabeth, running to the door. But just as she reached it, Mr. Darcy came in. Her pale face and strange manner prevented him from speaking, and she, who could think of nothing except Lydia, said hurriedly, "Excuse me, but I must leave you. I must find Mr. Gardiner immediately. There is not a moment to lose."

"Good God! What is the matter?" he cried, then added, "Let me, or let the servant, go to find Mr. and Mrs. Gardiner. You are not well enough. You cannot go yourself."

Elizabeth hesitated, but her legs were trembling, and she realized he was right. After giving the servant her message, she sat down, looking so ill that Darcy could not leave her or stop himself saying gently, "Let me call someone to look after you. Shall I get you a glass of wine? You are very ill."

"No, thank you," she replied. "I am quite well. I am only upset by some dreadful news I've just received from Longbourn." She burst into tears, and for a few minutes she could not speak another word. Darcy watched her miserably, in sympathetic silence. At last, she spoke again. "It cannot be hidden from anyone. My youngest sister has eloped, with—with Mr. Wickham. *You* know him too well to doubt what will happen. She has no money, no connections, nothing that can tempt him to marry her. She is lost for ever. And I could have prevented it! I knew how bad his character was. If only I had told my family what I knew about him! But it is all too late now."

Darcy looked at her in astonishment. "I am shocked," he said, "and sad, very sad. What has been done to find her and bring her back?"

"My father has gone to London, and I hope my uncle will go too. We shall leave Lambton, I hope, in half an hour. But I know very well that nothing can be done. How can such a man be persuaded? How can we even find them? I have not the smallest hope. It is horrible!"

Darcy made no answer. He was walking up and down with a serious, thoughtful expression on his face. Elizabeth soon observed and instantly understood it. She was losing her influence over him. This proof of moral weakness in her family was driving him away from her. Never before had she so honestly believed she could have loved him as now, when mutual affection must be impossible.

But she could not think for long of herself when Lydia's situation was so desperate. Mr. Darcy left almost immediately, politely regretting that Elizabeth and her aunt and uncle would not, in the circumstances, be able to come to dinner at Pemberley that day, and again expressing his sympathy. When Mr. and Mrs. Gardiner entered the room, Elizabeth hurriedly explained everything to them, and she was greatly relieved when they agreed to leave at once to return to Longbourn.

Their packing was done at great speed, and soon they were in the carriage, driving south.

"Lizzy," began Mrs. Gardiner, "I cannot believe that Wickham's character is so bad that he would run away with Lydia and not marry her. Do you really think he is capable of that?"

"My dear aunt, Jane and I both know that he has neither honesty nor honor. He has falsely accused Mr. Darcy and has lied wickedly about the whole Darcy family. You saw what a shy, gentle girl Miss Darcy is, but he had described her as proud, disagreeable, and disdainful."

"But does Lydia know nothing of this?"

"Oh, no! That is the worst of all. I didn't know the truth myself until my visit to Kent, and when I returned and told Jane, she and I decided not to make our knowledge public. Now I know that was a mistake. I never thought that Lydia could be in any danger from him."

When they arrived at Longbourn, Elizabeth and her aunt were able to help Jane in looking after the children. They also attempted to calm Mrs. Bennet, who, however, refused to be calmed and blamed everyone except herself for the disaster.

"If only I had been allowed to take the family to Brighton, this would not have happened. Poor dear Lydia had no one to take care of her. Why did those Forsters ever let her go out of their sight? I am sure they neglected her. Of course, I did not want her to go to Brighton, but nobody took any notice of me, as usual. And now Mr. Bennet has gone to London, and I'm sure he'll fight Wickham, and then he'll be killed, and then the Collinses will turn us out of the house, before he's cold in his grave!"

"Do not worry, sister," said Mr. Gardiner kindly. "I'm going to London tomorrow to help my brother-in-law."

"Oh, thank you, my dear brother," replied Mrs. Bennet. "Make sure you find Lydia and Wickham, and if they are not married yet, *make* them marry. And tell Lydia, they mustn't wait for wedding clothes, but she shall have as much money as she wants to buy them, after they are married. And keep Mr. Bennet from fighting—tell him what a dreadful state I am in, so ill that I can get no rest by night or by day. And tell Lydia not to buy any clothes until she's seen me because she doesn't know the best shops. Oh, brother, how kind you are! I hope you will manage everything."

The next day Mr. Gardiner traveled to London, as he had promised. Now began a painful period of waiting for those left at Longbourn. They became even more anxious, as news came from Meryton of Wickham's lies, debts, and secret attachments to most of the servant girls in the town. Everybody declared that he was the wickedest young man in the world and protested that they had always distrusted his great charm and appearance of goodness. Although Elizabeth did not believe half of these stories, she believed enough to feel sure that her sister's reputation was already lost, and even Jane almost despaired of receiving good news.

In a few days' time they were relieved to receive a letter from Mr. Gardiner, but unfortunately it only informed them that Wickham and Lydia had not yet been found. Apparently Wickham had left gambling debts of over a thousand pounds behind him in Brighton. Mr. Bennet was returning home the following day, leaving his brother-in-law in London to continue the search. When she heard this, Mrs. Bennet did not show as much satisfaction as her children expected, considering the anxiety she had previously expressed for her husband's safety.

"What, is he coming home without poor Lydia?" she cried. "And who will fight Wickham and make him marry her?"

Mrs. Gardiner took the opportunity of Mr. Bennet's return to go back to London herself, with her children. She was still longing to know how Elizabeth's relationship with Darcy had developed, but Elizabeth had not once mentioned his name, so her aunt did not dare to ask any direct questions.

When Mr. Bennet arrived home, he appeared as calm as ever, but in a conversation with Elizabeth he admitted that he felt to blame for Lydia's elopement.

"I know I should have had more control over her," he said. "And, Lizzy, you were right. I should never have let her go to Brighton."

Kitty, who was listening, said, "Papa, if *I* ever went to Brighton, I'd behave much better than Lydia has done."

"You go to Brighton!" cried her father. "I would not trust you within ten miles of the place, for fifty pounds! No, Kitty, I have at last learned to be cautious, and you will feel the effects of it. No officer may ever enter the house again, or even pass through the village. And balls will be absolutely forbidden unless you dance only with your sisters."

Kitty, taking these threats seriously, began to cry.

"Well, well," said he, "don't make yourself unhappy. If you are a good girl for the next ten years, I'll take you to the theater at the end of that time."

Two days later, the news for which they had all been waiting so anxiously arrived. Mr. Gardiner's letter informed them that Wickham and Lydia had been found, but that they were not married. However, certain financial arrangements had been made with Wickham. Mr. Bennet was asked to pay Lydia one hundred pounds a year, as well as arranging for her to inherit her equal share of the five thousand pounds which the Bennet girls would inherit after their parents' death. If these reasonable conditions were agreed, Wickham had promised to marry Lydia.

At first Elizabeth and Jane were delighted that their sister's reputation would be saved through marriage, even to such a man as Wickham. But then their father explained that Wickham would never have agreed to marry Lydia unless he had been paid a considerable amount of money immediately. They began to worry that it would be difficult to repay Mr. Gardiner, who must have bribed Wickham in this way. Mrs. Bennet, however, had no such worries.

"He is her own uncle, after all!" she cried happily. "Why shouldn't he pay? My dear, dear Lydia! Married at sixteen! How I long to see her, and dear Wickham too! But the wedding clothes! I'll write to my sister-in-law about them at once! I'm so happy. In a short time I'll have a daughter married. Mrs. Wickham! How well it sounds!"

Now that Lydia was going to be married, Elizabeth greatly regretted telling Darcy of her fears for her sister. But even if Lydia had been married in the most honorable way, it was extremely unlikely that Mr. Darcy would wish to connect himself with a family in which there was a close relationship with Wickham, the man he most justly disliked. She could not expect him to go on caring for her as she felt certain he had done when they met in Derbyshire. But now that she was sure he could not love her, she was convinced they could have been happy together. He seemed to be exactly the man who would have suited her. They could have usefully influenced each other. His mind might have been softened and his manners improved by her sociability, and she might have learned from his greater judgment and knowledge of the world. But no such relationship could now teach an admiring world what happiness in marriage was really like. Instead, Wickham would marry Lydia, with little chance of happiness for either of them.

Mr. and Mrs. Gardiner had arranged for Lydia to be married quietly in London, from their house. At first Mr. Bennet had refused to allow his youngest daughter ever to enter his house again, but eventually Jane and Elizabeth persuaded him to receive Lydia and her husband after the wedding. It would only be a short visit, as almost immediately she and Wickham would be moving north to Newcastle, where he had accepted a new army post.

When the carriage containing the young couple arrived at Longbourn House, the two elder Bennet sisters were shocked to see how unashamed Lydia was. She entered the house, laughing and joking, and asked all her sisters to congratulate her. Wickham was no more embarrassed than she was and spoke to everyone in his usual flattering, agreeable manner. They seemed to have no idea of the anxiety they had caused by their shameless and wicked behavior.

Elizabeth was quite disgusted by their relaxed, confident appearance and determined not to show any interest when

Lydia entered the house laughing,
and asked all her sisters to congratulate her.

Lydia insisted on describing every detail of her wedding day. She could not help reacting with astonishment, however, when Lydia let slip the name of Mr. Darcy. He had apparently been present at the ceremony. Why would Mr. Darcy, Elizabeth wondered, attend the wedding of two people he must hold in the greatest contempt? She could not discover the reason from Lydia, who suddenly remembered it was supposed to be a secret, and she could not rest without knowing the truth, so she hurriedly sent a note to her aunt in London, asking urgently for an explanation.

Bingley Returns to Netherfield

Elizabeth had the satisfaction of receiving a reply from her aunt in the shortest time possible. She sat down eagerly to read it.

My dear niece,

I must confess I am astonished by your request for information about Mr. Darcy's share in arranging Lydia's marriage. I assumed that you would know all about it. Your uncle is as surprised as I am. But if you are really innocent and ignorant, I must tell you all the details. On the day I returned to London from Longbourn, your uncle had a most unexpected visitor. Mr. Darcy came to tell us he had discovered where your sister and Wickham were staying. The reason he gave for wanting to help was his belief that he was to blame for not making Wickham's worthlessness more public, and that therefore it was his duty to assist us in every possible way. If he had *another* motive, I am sure it would be just as honorable. He knew that Wickham had a close friend in London, a woman who had once been companion to Miss Darcy, and who had been dismissed for some reason. So Mr. Darcy found this woman and bribed her to give him Wickham's present address.

He went to see Wickham and insisted on seeing Lydia, hoping to persuade her to return to her family. However, Lydia told him she only cared for Wickham and had no intention of leaving him, whether he married her or not. Wickham privately told Mr. Darcy that he had left the regiment because of his gambling debts, not because he intended to marry Lydia, and that he was still hoping to find and marry a woman of fortune in order to have a comfortable income. It was clearly necessary to persuade him to marry Lydia as soon as possible, and Mr. Darcy had several meetings with Wickham to arrange financial matters with him. Finally, Mr. Darcy was able to visit your uncle, as I have said, to explain the whole business and to insist that he alone should be responsible for paying Wickham the promised amount. Your uncle argued with him for a long time, but our visitor was so obstinate that Mr. Gardiner eventually had to agree. I think, Lizzy, that obstinacy is Mr. Darcy's real fault, rather than any of the other faults of which he has been accused. He paid Wickham several thousand pounds, for past debts and future expenses and attended the wedding to make a final payment. And in spite of Mr. Darcy's declared motives, my dear Lizzy, you may be sure that your uncle would never have given in if we had not assumed that Mr. Darcy had *another interest* in the matter. Will you be very angry with me, my dear Lizzy, if I take this opportunity of saying how much I like him? His behavior to us has always been as agreeable as when we were in Derbyshire. I think that if he marries *the right woman*, his wife may teach him to become more sociable. Please forgive me if I have assumed too much, or at least do not punish me by not inviting me to Pemberley. I shall never be happy until I have been all the way around the park.

But I must go to my children now.
Yours very sincerely,
M. Gardiner

Elizabeth read this letter with a mixture of pleasure and pain.
Mr. Darcy had thought so little of his pride that he had spent
considerable time, effort, and money on two people for whom
he must feel the greatest disdain. He had even had to bargain
with Wickham! She could not believe he had done all this for
her, a woman who had already rejected him. But the fact
remained that she and her family owed him everything. How
bitterly she now regretted criticizing and mocking him in the
past! She was ashamed of herself, but she was proud of him,
proud that in a matter of honor he had been able to conquer
his own pride. She was even rather pleased, if a little regretful,
that her aunt and uncle had felt sure that there was mutual
affection between Mr. Darcy and herself.

Mrs. Bennet was quite depressed when Lydia and Wickham
left Longbourn to travel north to Newcastle. But soon Mrs.
Philips brought the happy news that Mr. Bingley was expected
to return to Netherfield in a day or two, and Mrs. Bennet became
very excited. She made preparations to invite him to dinner and
counted the days that must pass before she could send the
invitation.

However, on only the third morning after his arrival, she
caught sight of him from her bedroom window, riding towards
Longbourn House with another gentleman, also on horseback.

"Girls! Quickly!" she cried. "Mr. Bingley is coming! And
who's that with him? It must be Mr. Darcy, that tall, proud man.
Well, as he is Mr. Bingley's friend, we must be polite to him, but
I must say, I hate the sight of him."

Both Jane and Elizabeth felt uncomfortable and sympathized with each other. Jane was nervous about meeting Bingley again and determined not to show her feelings. Elizabeth was uneasy at the thought of seeing Darcy as she was the only one who knew how much the whole family owed him in spite of their general dislike of him. She was astonished that he had come to see her, and for a moment she allowed herself to hope that his affection and wishes might still be the same.

She was disappointed, however, by the visit. Mr. Darcy said scarcely anything to her and appeared more thoughtful and less anxious to please than in Derbyshire. She wondered bitterly why he had come. In addition, she was highly embarrassed by her mother's behavior. With flattering smiles Mrs. Bennet concentrated all her conversation on Mr. Bingley while throwing the occasional unpleasant remark in Mr. Darcy's direction. The only positive effect of the gentlemen's visit was the way in which Jane's charm and beauty appeared to excite Mr. Bingley's admiration all over again, which Elizabeth was relieved and delighted to see.

The Bennet family did not see the two gentlemen again until Tuesday when they came to dinner at Longbourn. It was a great pleasure to Elizabeth to watch Bingley sitting beside Jane and talking happily to her, but this was the only enjoyment she gained from the party. Mr. Darcy was unfortunately sitting a long way from her, next to Mrs. Bennet. Elizabeth could see how seldom they spoke to each other and how cold and formal their behavior to each other was. She would have given anything to be able to tell him that his kindness was appreciated by at least one of the family. All through the long dinner, she desperately hoped there would be an opportunity for her to have some real conversation with him later. But the evening passed without any more than a short exchange of politeness between them, and Elizabeth lost all hope of immediate happiness.

Two days after this, Mr. Bingley called at Longbourn House again. This time he was alone as Mr. Darcy had gone to London. He sat with the ladies for over an hour, talking cheerfully and agreeably to them. He came the next morning, and again in the evening. Mrs. Bennet took every opportunity to leave him alone with Jane, by calling her other daughters out of the room for some reason or other. She was hoping to encourage him to propose, but in spite of her efforts Bingley remained charming, agreeable, and unattached.

But on the third day Bingley came in the morning to go shooting with Mr. Bennet. He stayed for lunch and was still there in the evening. And when Elizabeth entered the sitting-room unexpectedly, to her surprise she saw Jane and Bingley standing close together near the fire. They turned hurriedly when they heard her and moved awkwardly away from each other. Bingley whispered something to Jane and ran out of the room. Jane could not keep her secret from her sister and, kissing her, cried, "I am the happiest creature in the world! Oh, Lizzy! I do not deserve this! Why isn't everybody as happy as I am!"

Elizabeth congratulated her sister most warmly and sincerely. "At last!" she thought. "The end of all Mr. Darcy's anxious advice! The end of all Caroline Bingley's lies and plans! The happiest, wisest, most reasonable end!"

"I must go and tell my mother," continued Jane, "as he has just gone to ask my father's permission. Oh, Lizzy! What happiness!"

It was a joyful evening for all of them. Jane looked more beautiful than ever, and Bingley was clearly very much in love. Mrs. Bennet could not say enough to describe her delight although she talked of nothing else all evening, and Mr. Bennet was evidently very pleased.

Before the two eldest sisters went to bed that night, Elizabeth listened willingly to Jane's long description of Bingley's good qualities. At the end, Jane added, "Oh, Lizzy! If only I could see *you* as happy as I am! If only there were another man like Bingley for *you*!"

"Dear Jane, I can never be as happy as you because I'm not as good as you. No, no, let me find my own husband. Perhaps, if I'm very lucky, I may meet another Mr. Collins one day."

The engagement was not kept a secret for very long. Mrs. Bennet whispered the news to Mrs. Philips, who told all her neighbors in Meryton. Everybody soon agreed that the Bennets were the luckiest family in the world although only a few weeks before, when Lydia had run away, they had been considered the most unfortunate.

Elizabeth and Darcy

One morning, about a week after Bingley had proposed to Jane, a carriage arrived outside Longbourn House. Elizabeth, Kitty, and their mother were in the sitting-room when suddenly the door was thrown open and their visitor entered. It was Lady Catherine de Bourgh.

They were all extremely astonished. Mrs. Bennet, flattered to have such an important visitor, received her with great politeness. After sitting for a moment in silence, Lady Catherine said very stiffly to Elizabeth, "I hope you are well, Miss Bennet.

That lady, I suppose, is your mother. And *that*, I suppose, is one of your sisters."

Elizabeth replied that she was correct in thinking so. Lady Catherine rose and said, "I would like to have a walk in your garden, Miss Bennet, if you would accompany me."

"Go, my dear," cried Mrs. Bennet. "Show her ladyship the different walks. I'm sure she will like them."

As they passed through the hall, Lady Catherine opened the doors into the different rooms, looked in, and declared them to be reasonable-looking rooms. They went into the garden in silence. Elizabeth was determined to make no effort at conversation with a woman who was being more than usually rude and disagreeable.

Lady Catherine began speaking when she was sure they were alone. "You must know, Miss Bennet, why I have come."

Elizabeth looked surprised. "Indeed, you are mistaken, madam. I have no idea why you are honoring us with a visit."

"Miss Bennet," replied her ladyship angrily, "however insincere you may be, you shall not find *me* so. A most alarming report reached me two days ago. I was told that *you*, Miss Elizabeth Bennet, would soon be engaged to my nephew, my own nephew, Mr. Darcy. Although I knew it must be a shameful lie and I would not offend him by supposing it to be possible, I decided at once to come here, to let you know my feelings."

"If you believed it to be impossible," said Elizabeth, with disdain, "I wonder why your ladyship took the trouble of coming so far."

"I came to insist on having this report contradicted. Tell me, is it true?"

"Your ladyship may ask questions which I shall not choose to answer."

"This is too much! Miss Bennet, I insist on an answer. Has my nephew made you an offer of marriage?"

"Your ladyship has declared it to be impossible."

"It *ought* to be impossible, but your skilful charms may have made him forget, in a moment of foolishness, what he owes to himself and his family. You *must* tell me. I am almost his nearest relation, and I have a right to know his plans."

"But you have no right to know *mine*."

"Let me speak plainly. This marriage, which you dare to hope for, can never take place because Mr. Darcy is engaged to *my daughter*. His mother and I planned their marriage when they were still children. They are an ideal couple, both from respectable, honorable, ancient families, with an excellent fortune on both sides. What can possibly divide them? The desperate ambitions of a young woman without family, connections or fortune? It cannot be! And I warn you, Miss Bennet, if you marry him, do not expect to be noticed by his family or friends. Your name will never even be mentioned by any of us."

"These are heavy misfortunes, but the wife of Mr. Darcy must necessarily be so happy that she could not regret her marriage."

"Obstinate girl! Tell me, are you engaged to him?"

Elizabeth could not avoid saying, after a moment's thought, "I am not."

Lady Catherine seemed pleased. "And will you promise me never to enter into such an engagement?"

"I will make no such promise. You have totally misunderstood my character if you think I can be persuaded by such threats. I do not know whether your nephew would approve of your interference in his life, but you certainly have no right to interfere in mine."

"To all the objections I have mentioned, I add one more. I am aware of your younger sister's elopement. Is *such* a girl to be my nephew's sister-in-law and bring shame on the ancient name of Darcy?"

"You can now have nothing more to say," Elizabeth said coldly. "You have insulted me in every possible way." She rose and started walking back to the house. Lady Catherine also rose and walked with her.

"Unfeeling, selfish girl! So you are determined to have him?"

"I have not said that. I am only determined to do what in *my* opinion will bring me happiness, without reference to *you*."

"Do not imagine, Miss Bennet, that you will ever achieve your ambition." When they arrived at her carriage, she added, "I send no compliments to your mother. You do not deserve such politeness. I am most seriously displeased."

Elizabeth did not answer and entered the house while Lady Catherine drove away in her carriage. She had to tell a little lie to her mother to explain Lady Catherine's unexpected visit and speedy departure, and then she shut herself in her room to consider what it all meant. Perhaps the Collinses had imagined, after the news of Jane's engagement to Bingley, that Darcy might marry *her*. They must have told Lady Catherine, who had made a special journey to Longbourn in order to break off this supposed engagement. Elizabeth began to feel depressed. If, as seemed likely, Lady Catherine now went straight to London to talk to her nephew, she might easily convince him of the inferiority of Elizabeth's social position. He would probably feel that his aunt's objections, which to Elizabeth appeared laughably weak, contained much common sense. In that case he might make up his mind not to marry her under any circumstances and to keep away from Longbourn altogether.

"You have insulted me in every possible way."

The next morning Mr. Bennet called Elizabeth into the library. In his hand he had a letter, which he had just received.

"Lizzy, I did not know I had *two* daughters about to be married. I congratulate you on a very important conquest."

Elizabeth blushed, thinking that Darcy himself had written.

"You seem to know what I mean, but I think even *you* will

not be able to guess your admirer's name. This letter is from Mr. Collins, and he first congratulates me on Jane's engagement, of which the gossiping Lucases have told him. Apparently the Lucases also think that my daughter Elizabeth might soon be marrying one of the great gentlemen in the country—Mr. Darcy, in fact! Now, Lizzy, I think I *have* surprised you. Could he have chosen anyone we know as a more unlikely husband for you? Mr. Darcy, who never praises, only criticizes women, and who probably never looked at you in his life! What an admirable choice!"

Elizabeth tried to share her father's amusement, but had never appreciated his humor so little.

"He goes on to say that when he dutifully gave this news to her ladyship, she made many objections and stated that she would never agree to the marriage. He kindly gives us this information, he says, to prevent his cousin Elizabeth and her admirer from rushing into a marriage not approved by their families. Well, Lizzy! What do you think of that? I do enjoy Mr. Collins' letters. And I am delighted the Lucases thought of Mr. Darcy. His perfect indifference to *you*, and your strong dislike of *him*, make it so extremely amusing. Don't you agree?"

Elizabeth had great difficulty in pretending to be amused by the letter. It was necessary to laugh when she would rather have cried. Her father had most cruelly hurt her by speaking of Darcy's indifference, and she began to wonder whether perhaps, instead of *his* seeing too little, *she* might have imagined too much.

In spite of Elizabeth's doubts, however, Mr. Darcy returned to Netherfield a few days later, and he and Mr. Bingley came to Longbourn soon afterwards. Bingley suggested they should all go for a walk, and while he and Jane concentrated on their own private conversation, some distance away, Elizabeth found herself alone with Mr. Darcy.

Taking a deep breath, she said bravely, "Mr. Darcy, I can no longer stop myself from thanking you for your extraordinary kindness to my poor sister. If the rest of my family knew of it, they would add their grateful thanks to mine."

"I had hoped to keep it a secret," he answered, "but if you must thank me, let it be for yourself alone. I shall not attempt to deny that wishing to give happiness to you was one of my reasons for helping your sister. But your *family* owe me nothing. Much as I respect them, I believe I thought only of *you*."

Elizabeth was too embarrassed to say a word. After a short pause he added, "You are too generous to play with my feelings. If you still feel as you did last April, tell me so at once. *My* affections and wishes are unchanged, but one word from you will prevent me from ever mentioning them again."

Elizabeth forced herself to speak, and immediately, though hesitatingly, gave him to understand that her feelings had changed so considerably since that time that she was now grateful and pleased to accept his proposal. When Darcy heard this, he was probably happier than he had ever been before, and he expressed himself as warmly and sensibly as a man violently in love can.

They walked on without noticing in which direction. There was so much to be thought, felt, and said. She soon learned that his aunt had indeed seen him in London after her disappointing visit to Longbourn. But unluckily for her ladyship, her critical comments and description of her conversation with Elizabeth produced exactly the opposite result to what she had intended.

"It taught me to hope," Darcy explained, "as I had hardly

ever allowed myself to hope before. I knew that if you had decided never to marry me, you would have admitted it to Lady Catherine openly and honestly."

Elizabeth blushed and laughed as she replied, "Yes, you have experienced my honesty. After scolding you so rudely to your face, I was obviously quite capable of criticizing you to all your relations."

"I certainly deserved all your accusations. As an only son, I was brought up to be selfish and proud, and to consider myself superior to others. I would have continued like that if you, dearest, loveliest Elizabeth, had not taught me a lesson. I owe you a great deal for that."

"And I, how soon I thought better of you when I read the letter you sent me! When I realized your description of events must be true, all my prejudices against you were removed!"

They talked of their unexpected meeting at Pemberley, which had renewed their interest in each other, of Georgiana Darcy's immediate liking for Elizabeth, and of the engagement between Jane and Bingley.

"I guessed," smiled Elizabeth, "that you had given your permission for their marriage."

"My permission! No! But I must admit I confessed to Bingley that I had made a mistake in supposing that your sister was indifferent to him, and I encouraged him to return to Netherfield to see if she still cared for him. I am delighted to hear of their engagement. He will be one of the happiest men in the world when he marries your sister. Only *I* shall be happier than him when I am fortunate enough to marry *you*."

Their conversation continued in this way until they suddenly became aware of the lateness of the hour. They returned to Longbourn House, where they separated.

That evening Elizabeth could not help telling Jane her news. However, she almost regretted doing so when she saw the astonishment on Jane's face. At first Jane could not believe that her sister was engaged to a man she had so disliked, and she wondered if Elizabeth could really be happy with him. But when she had been convinced by Elizabeth's explanations and promises, she was delighted and congratulated her sister with all her heart.

The next day Mr. Darcy came to ask Mr. Bennet officially for Elizabeth's hand in marriage. Mr. Bennet also had to be persuaded that his favorite daughter could really be happy with such a proud, disdainful man. Only Mrs. Bennet did not need to be convinced, although she was, most unusually, speechless with shock when she heard the news. When she recovered a little, she cried, "My sweetest Lizzy! How rich you will be! What jewels, what carriages you will have! Mr. Darcy! Such a charming man! So handsome! So tall! I am so sorry I disliked him before. Ten thousand a year! Oh, my dear Lizzy!"

During the weeks of her engagement, Elizabeth was glad to see that all her family were beginning to appreciate Mr. Darcy's good qualities. Determined to protect him from her mother's overfamiliarity, she was relieved to see that Mrs. Bennet respected her future son-in-law too much to say more than a few words to him. In spite of this, Elizabeth looked happily forward to the time when she and Darcy would leave Longbourn and move to all the comfort and elegance of their own home at Pemberley.

Mrs. Bennet was a happy mother indeed on the day when she got rid of her two most deserving daughters. It may be guessed with what delighted pride she afterwards visited Mrs. Bingley and talked of Mrs. Darcy. Mr. Bennet missed his second daughter very much and greatly enjoyed going to Pemberley to visit her.

Mr. Bingley and Jane stayed only a year at Netherfield before buying a large house in the north, only thirty miles from Pemberley. In this way, the two sisters were permitted their dearest wish and were able to visit each other frequently.

Mary was the only sister who remained at home as Kitty spent most of her time with her two elder sisters, which greatly improved her behavior, character, and intelligence.

Lydia and Wickham were always moving from one place to another in search of cheap rooms, and always spending more than they should. His affection for her soon became indifference while hers for him lasted a little longer. They were not too proud to ask Lydia's sisters for financial help during every crisis, and Elizabeth and Jane both sent them regular gifts of money to pay their bills.

Caroline Bingley was deeply offended by Darcy's marriage, but she did not show her bitterness and was always extremely polite to Elizabeth. Georgiana Darcy, on the other hand, became greatly attached to Elizabeth and had the highest opinion of her. Lady Catherine, however, was so rude about Elizabeth to her nephew that he broke off communication completely with her for a time. In the end Elizabeth persuaded him to forgive his aunt, who eventually forgot her pride enough to visit them at Pemberley.

There remained a close relationship between the Darcys and the Gardiners. Darcy and Elizabeth were both warmly grateful to the two people who, by inviting her to Derbyshire and taking her to visit Pemberley, had brought them together.

GLOSSARY

accomplished well trained or educated in social skills such as conversation, art, music, etc.

affection a strong feeling of liking or love

agreeable pleasant, charming

amends, make amends to put right a mistake or an injustice done to somebody

apparent seeming, not real

astonishment great surprise

attachment a feeling of liking or love for a place or person

ball a grand, formal dance

blush (*v*) to become red in the face, especially when embarrassed

the Church the Church of England

colonel an army title; the head of a regiment

compliment (*n* and *v*) a remark expressing respect or admiration

conquer to repress or control; (*n*) **conquest**

considerate thoughtful; careful not to hurt other people's feelings

contempt a feeling that someone or something is worthless

desire (*n*) a strong wish

disdain (*n*) a feeling or show of superiority or dislike

elder/eldest older/oldest (used only of people, especially of members of a family)

elegance good taste in clothes, appearance, and manner

elope to run away from home in order to get married secretly

favorable giving or showing approval

flatter (*v*) to praise someone too much or insincerely

gentleman a man of good family and social position, usually wealthy

haste a hurry; quickness of action

honor (*n*)   moral principles; a privilege or pleasure

indifference   a complete lack of concern or interest

inferior   less clever or important than other people, or of lower social position

justice   right and fair behavior or treatment

ladyship   a title used in speaking to or about a titled lady

late   no longer alive

library   a room in a house, used for keeping books

long (*v*)   to want to do something very much

master, mistress   a man or woman who owns a house and employs servants

mock (*v*)   to laugh unkindly at someone, to make fun of them

morals   an understanding of right and wrong behavior

mutual   of a feeling shared by two people

obstinate   refusing to change one's opinion or actions; (*n*) **obstinacy**

party   a group of people doing something together

patron   (here) a person who has the right to give someone a Church of England post (e.g., the post of rector)

penniless   very poor; having no money at all

propose   to ask someone to marry you

rector   a priest in the Church of England

rectory   a rector's house

regiment   a large number of soldiers, part of an army

reject (*v*)   to refuse to accept

right (*n*)   a proper claim to something

servility   being too ready to obey other people and behave like a servant

sister/brother-in-law   a sister/brother by marriage (e.g., your husband's sister)

sociable   fond of being with other people; friendly

superior better, cleverer, more important than other people, or of higher social position

taste (here) the ability to enjoy or to choose things which are elegant, attractive, and pleasing

underestimate (*v*) to have too low an opinion of something or someone

vulgar low, common, coarse, lacking in taste or manners

ACTIVITIES

Before Reading

1 **Read the back cover of the book and the story introduction on the first page. Can you guess which of these ideas are true?**

1 Mr. Darcy is a proud man because . . .
   a) he has achieved a great deal in his life.
   b) he feels socially superior to other people.

2 Elizabeth Bennet is prejudiced against Mr. Darcy because . . .
   a) she has been given false information about him.
   b) she cannot make reasoned judgements about anyone.

3 This story about the Bennet family is likely to include . . .
   a) misunderstandings   e) parties and dances
   b) quarrels   f) despair and death
   c) jealousy   g) interfering friends
   d) political events   h) war and battles

2 **Read these two quotes from the story introduction on the first page, and choose the most probable meaning for each one.**

1 "It is a truth well known to all the world that an unmarried man in possession of a large fortune must be in need of a wife."
   a) A rich man needs a wife to look after him and his money.
   b) A rich man makes an attractive husband.

2 "And even better, he loves dancing! Everybody knows that means he's likely to fall in love!"
   a) Dancing is a good way of showing off female charms and attracting a man's interest.
   b) Men who love dancing always fall in love.

ACTIVITIES

While Reading

Read Chapters 1 to 4. Who said this, and to whom? What, or who, were they talking about?

1 "So you must visit him as soon as he arrives."
2 "I didn't expect it at all!"
3 "A lady's imagination jumps from admiration, to love, to marriage, in a moment."
4 "I've suspected it for some time, but now I'm convinced."
5 "You'd better ride over there because it looks likely to rain . . ."
6 "She has no conversation, no elegance, and no beauty!"
7 "*I* think it shows a very pleasing affection for her sister."
8 "I have come prepared to admire the young ladies. And perhaps when we know each other better—"
9 "I've spent four days in the same house as him, and I consider him very disagreeable."
10 "When the post became vacant, it was given to somebody else."
11 "You could remark on the size of the room or the number of couples."
12 "Whether he can *keep* them is less certain."

Before you read Chapter 5 (*Mr. Collins Proposes Twice*), can you guess the answers to these questions?

1 Who will Mr. Collins propose to?
2 Will he propose to the same girl twice, or to two different girls?
3 Will anybody accept him, and if so, who?

**Read Chapters 5 to 7. Are these sentences true (T) or false (F)?
Rewrite the false sentences with the correct information.**

1 When Elizabeth rejected him, Mr. Collins was sure she would
   accept him the next time he proposed.
2 Mr. and Mrs. Bennet agreed in their opinion of Mr. Collins.
3 Caroline Bingley hoped her brother would marry Jane Bennet.
4 Charlotte Lucas was happy to accept Mr. Collins' proposal.
5 Jane was only slightly disappointed at Mr. Bingley's failure to
   return to Netherfield.
6 Mrs. Gardiner gave Elizabeth some sensible advice about
   Wickham.
7 Charlotte spent as much time as possible with her new
   husband.
8 Lady Catherine was a polite, charming woman, and sensitive
   to other people's feelings.
9 Colonel Fitzwilliam needed to marry a girl with a fortune.
10 Darcy denied doing his best to separate Bingley and Jane.
11 If Darcy had made his proposal to Elizabeth more flattering,
   she would have accepted him.

**Before you read Chapter 8 (*Elizabeth Learns More about Darcy and
Wickham*), what do you think is going to happen? Circle Y (Yes)
or N (No) for each of these possibilities.**

1 Elizabeth learns something that makes her change her mind
   about Wickham. Y/N
2 Darcy proves to Elizabeth that he had good reasons for his
   actions. Y/N
3 Elizabeth discovers that Darcy is even prouder and more cruel
   than she thought. Y/N

Read Chapters 8 to 11. Choose the best question-word for these questions, and then answer them.

Why / What / Who

1 . . . reasons did Darcy give for objecting to Bingley's attachment to Jane?
2 . . . had Darcy paid Wickham three thousand pounds?
3 . . . did Wickham want to elope with Georgiana Darcy?
4 . . . did Elizabeth feel ashamed after reading Darcy's letter?
5 . . . was invited by the Colonel's wife to go to Brighton?
6 . . . went on holiday to Derbyshire?
7 . . . was Elizabeth surprised by the Pemberley housekeeper's description of Mr. Darcy?
8 . . . did Darcy want to introduce to Elizabeth?
9 . . . was the Bennet family's worst fear, when they discovered Lydia had eloped with Wickham?
10 . . . did Elizabeth blame herself for Lydia's elopement?
11 . . . persuaded Wickham to marry Lydia?
12 . . . did Mrs. Gardiner think Darcy's real motive was?
13 . . . knew the truth about Lydia's and Wickham's marriage?
14 . . . new secret was soon known all around Meryton?

Before you read Chapter 12 (*Elizabeth and Darcy*), can you guess the answer to these questions?

1 Will Darcy propose to Elizabeth again, and will she accept him?
2 Who tries to prevent a possible engagement between Darcy and Elizabeth?
3 If they do get engaged, how will their families and friends react to the news?

After Reading

1 Here are some quotes from ten characters in the story. Decide who said or wrote each one, and then explain what the remark shows about each character.

1 "I think it's better to know as little as possible about the person you're going to spend your life with."

2 "If your daughter should become seriously ill and die, it would be a comfort to know that she died in a good cause, and in obedience to your orders."

3 "You know how I hate dancing with a partner I don't know. I would particularly dislike it at a village dance like this."

4 "Never in my life have I witnessed such considerate behavior in a person of high birth!"

5 "Nobody is more beautiful, elegant or accomplished than Georgiana Darcy. Louisa and I have great affection for her, and hope one day to call her sister."

6 "I have nothing to complain of, as he made no promises to me. I just thought he cared for me, but I was wrong."

7 "Such a charming man! So handsome! So tall! I am so sorry I disliked him before. Ten thousand a year! Oh, my dear Lizzy!"

8 "I warn you, Miss Bennet, if you marry him, do not expect to be noticed by his family or friends. Your name will never even be mentioned by any of us."

9 "I cannot promise what I will do, but I will really try to do what I think is wisest."

10 "Mr. Darcy has behaved wickedly towards me, but I could forgive him anything except the insult to his father's memory."

2 **Darcy found Wickham in London and persuaded him to marry Lydia (see page 91). Here is the conversation between the two men. Complete Darcy's side of the conversation.**

WICKHAM: So, Darcy, you've discovered our hiding-place! And what are you going to do about it?

DARCY: _____

WICKHAM: Marry her? Why should I? No, we've had some fun together, but I need to find a woman of fortune to marry.

DARCY: _____

WICKHAM: Oh, I imagine she'll go back to her silly mother. I can't worry about that—I've got my debts to take care of.

DARCY: _____

WICKHAM: Well, at least four thousand pounds. But why do you ask?

DARCY: _____

WICKHAM: I'm afraid it's not tempting enough, Darcy. That would only pay my debts, and I'd need much more than that. Marriage is an expensive business, you know.

DARCY: _____

WICKHAM: For that amount of money, yes, I'll marry her! She'll be delighted! But Darcy, tell me, what's your reason for doing this?

DARCY: _____

WICKHAM: Well, it is my business in a way. Because why are you paying me a large sum of money to marry a girl who has no connection with you? Ah, perhaps you have an interest in—

DARCY: _____

WICKHAM: All right, all right, I won't name her. But I think I've discovered your secret, Darcy. I congratulate you on your choice. A charming woman, and with your wealth, you don't need to worry about her lack of fortune!

3 **Imagine that Elizabeth replied to Darcy's letter (page 68). Here is the beginning of her letter. Complete it in the same style, and choose a final sentence from the three possible ones given below. Explain why you think your chosen sentence is the best one.**

Dear Mr. Darcy,

I am writing in response to your letter, the contents of which, I must confess, I found extremely disturbing. Before I received your letter, I was certain I knew the circumstances surrounding Mr. Bingley's separation from Jane, and I was also sure I had judged Mr. Wickham's character correctly. Now I must admit I was wrong . . .

Possible final sentences:
1 I am grateful to you for correcting my understanding of the facts, and I wish you all happiness in the future.
2 I hope that, now that these misunderstandings between us have been removed, we may at least be able to take pleasure in each other's conversation if we happen to meet socially in future.
3 You have shown yourself to be a man of honor and feeling, and I deeply regret my angry and ungenerous response to your proposal of marriage. If I had known then what I know now, I might have replied very differently.

4 **Here are parts of four letters written by different people, after hearing the news of Elizabeth's engagement to Mr. Darcy. Decide who wrote them, and to whom (the names are given below), and choose one suitable word to fill each gap.**

Lydia / Jane / Caroline Bingley / Mr. Bennet / Mrs. Louisa Hurst / Mrs. Bennet / Mr. Collins / Mrs. Gardiner

1 This news, my dear _____, has made me very _____. I was so

sure _____ intended to propose to _____! I would be the _____
of Pemberley now, if _____ had never met that _____ Bennet
girl. I really _____ her! And such a _____ family!

2 My dear, it's such _____ news, don't you think? _____ will have
the most _____ dresses and jewels! I _____ thought little Lizzy
would _____ Mr. Darcy, who is _____ than Mr. Bingley! If _____
cannot pay all his _____, I'm sure you can _____ your sister for
some _____.

3 Dear Sir, I must _____ you once more for _____. Elizabeth will
very soon _____ the wife of Mr. _____. Comfort Lady Catherine
as _____ as you can. But _____ I were you, I _____ take the
nephew's side. _____ has more to give.

4 There is nothing that _____ add more to my _____ than this
news! She's _____ in love with him. _____ he isn't like my _____
Bingley (no man could _____!), I know she'll be _____ with
him. You have _____ him already, haven't you?

5 **What are *your* opinions on marriage? Discuss these questions.**

1 "Happiness in marriage is simply a question of chance," said
Charlotte Lucas. Do you agree? Why, or why not?

2 "I made up my mind to save my friend from what I considered
would be a most unhappy marriage," wrote Darcy. Should
people interfere in their friends' love lives? Why, or why not?

3 "You would disappoint your father by agreeing to marry a
penniless young man," said Mrs. Gardiner. Is money, or the
lack of it, important in a marriage? Why, or why not?

4 Which of the four marriages in this story will be the most
successful, and the least successful? Explain why you think this.

ABOUT THE AUTHOR

Jane Austen was born in 1775 at Steventon in Hampshire, in the south of England. She was the sixth of seven children of a clergyman, the Reverend George Austen. He was a well-educated man, who encouraged Jane both in her reading and her writing. In 1801 the family moved to Bath; then, after George Austen's death, to Southampton, and finally to Chawton in Hampshire (the house where Jane lived can still be visited). She led a quiet, uneventful life, occasionally visiting London, Bath, Lyme, and her brothers' houses. She never married, though she had several admirers. One proposal of marriage she accepted, but the next day she changed her mind and withdrew her acceptance. Little is known about her love affairs, as her sister Cassandra was careful to edit Jane's private letters after her death, but it seems likely that Jane experienced disappointment in love and that she refused to marry without it. However, her life was spent in a close and affectionate family circle, and she was a much-loved aunt to her many nieces and nephews. She died in Winchester in 1817, aged only forty-two.

She started writing when she was only fourteen, and by her early twenties was already working on the first versions of some of her novels. She did not write about great events, like the French Revolution or the Napoleonic Wars, both of which happened during her lifetime. She wrote about what she knew best—the daily business of social visits, romantic affairs, and matchmaking. In a letter to a niece she wrote, "Three or four families in a country village is the very thing to work on." And in a reply to a suggestion for the subject of her next novel, she explained that she could not write anything without "laughing at myself or at other people." With characteristic modesty she finished, "No, I must keep to my own style and go on in my own way; and though I may never succeed again in that, I am convinced that I should totally fail in any other."

Her six major novels are now classics of English literature. They are *Sense and Sensibility, Pride and Prejudice, Mansfield Park, Emma, Northanger Abbey,* and *Persuasion.* Of these, *Mansfield Park, Emma,* and *Persuasion* were written in the busy parlor at Chawton, in the middle of all the usual family activities and interruptions. *Pride and Prejudice,* originally called *First Impressions,* was rejected without being read by the publisher, but it was rewritten and finally published in 1813. Elizabeth Bennet was Jane Austen's favorite heroine. "I must confess that I think her as delightful a creature as ever appeared in print," she wrote to her sister Cassandra. All her novels were praised for their wit and style by readers of the time, and the Prince Regent (later King George IV) enjoyed them so much that he kept a complete set of her novels in each of his houses.

The novels have remained popular since they were first published, and there is a Jane Austen Society (known as the Janeites), which guards her literary reputation and her memory jealously. There have been film and television dramatizations of all the novels, in particular some very successful recent films of *Pride and Prejudice, Emma,* and *Sense and Sensibility.*

Jane Austen is one of the greatest novelists in the English language. Her novels are comedies of manners, dealing with parties, dresses, quarrels, engagements, and marriages, but no writer has ever drawn "such pictures of domestic life in country villages" with a sharper eye or with a more exquisite irony.

OXFORD BOOKWORMS LIBRARY

Classics • Crime & Mystery • Factfiles • Fantasy & Horror
Human Interest • Playscripts • Thriller & Adventure
True Stories • World Stories

The OXFORD BOOKWORMS LIBRARY provides enjoyable reading in English, with a wide range of classic and modern fiction, non-fiction, and plays. It includes original and adapted texts in seven carefully graded language stages which take learners from beginner to advanced level.

All Stage 1 titles, as well as over eighty other titles from Starter to Stage 6, are available as audio recordings. All Starters and many titles at Stages 1 to 4 are specially recommended for younger learners. Every Bookworm is illustrated, and Starters and Factfiles have full-color illustrations.

The OXFORD BOOKWORMS LIBRARY also offers extensive support. Each book contains an introduction to the story, notes about the author, a glossary, and activities. Additional resources include tests and worksheets, as well as answers for these and for the activities in the books. There is advice on running a class library, using audio recordings, and the many ways of using Oxford Bookworms in reading programs. Resource materials are available on the website <www.oup.com/bookworms>.

The *Oxford Bookworms Collection* is a series for advanced learners. It consists of volumes of short stories by well-known authors, both classic and modern. Texts are not abridged or adapted in any way, but carefully selected to be accessible to the advanced student.

You can find details and a full list of titles in the *Oxford Bookworms Library Catalog* and *Oxford English Language Teaching Catalogs*, and on the website <www.oup.com/bookworms>.

BOOKWORMS · CLASSICS · STAGE 4

A Tale of Two Cities

CHARLES DICKENS

Retold by Ralph Mowat

"The Marquis lay there, like stone, with a knife pushed into his heart. On his chest lay a piece of paper, with the words: *Drive him fast to the grave. This is from JACQUES.*"

The French Revolution brings terror and death to many people. But even in these troubled times people can still love and be kind. They can be generous, true-hearted . . . and brave.

BOOKWORMS · CLASSICS · STAGE 5

Great Expectations

CHARLES DICKENS

Retold by Clare West

In a gloomy, neglected house Miss Havisham sits—as she has sat year after year—in a wedding dress and veil that were once white and are now faded and yellow with age. Her face is like a death's head; her dark eyes burn with bitterness and hate. By her side sits a proud and beautiful girl, and in front of her, trembling with fear in his thick country boots, stands young Pip.

Miss Havisham stares at Pip coldly and murmurs to the girl at her side, "Break his heart, Estella. Break his heart!"

BOOKWORMS · CLASSICS · STAGE 5

Wuthering Heights

EMILY BRONTË

Retold by Clare West

The wind is strong on the Yorkshire moors. There are few trees and fewer houses to block its path. There is one house, however, that does not hide from the wind. It stands out from the hill and challenges the wind to do its worst. The house is called Wuthering Heights.

When Mr. Earnshaw brings a strange, small, dark child back home to Wuthering Heights, it seems he has opened his doors to trouble. He has invited in something that, like the wind, is safer kept out of the house.

BOOKWORMS · CLASSICS · STAGE 6

Oliver Twist

CHARLES DICKENS

Retold by Richard Rogers

London in the 1830s was no place to be if you were a hungry ten-year-old boy, an orphan without friends or family, with no home to go to, and with only a penny in your pocket to buy a piece of bread.

But Oliver Twist finds some friends—Fagin, the Artful Dodger, and Charley Bates. They give him food and shelter and play games with him, but it is not until some days later that Oliver finds out what kind of friends they are and what kind of "games" they play . . .